'We Never Said Goodbye'

A Memoir

By Chloe Whyte

Table of Contents

Special Note From The Author

Grief varies from person to person; the journey of grief can feel awfully dark and lonely.

Grief isn't a little bump in the road, a blip if you like. It's not something that we all just "get over". The effect of a loved one's death leaves a wound in your heart that never fully heals.

You will always have those scars reminding you, and you'll always miss your loved one every single day.

While everyone experiences grief differently, what we all have in common is the understanding that getting back to our previous lives is the hardest and longest journey that we will ever experience.

This book is for anyone who has lost someone in their life, whether it's a parent, a child, a sibling, a partner, a best friend, anyone. Although I am no doctor or therapist, I have experienced the loss of a loved one.

I wrote this book to help others know that they're not alone. At first you will feel as if you are going through this dark, empty cave solo. You will think that you'll never be happy again, but one day you will learn how to be happy again.

Everyone copes with grief differently; there is no time limit – please remember that.

Some of us will experience many emotions and it's a hell of a ride. Some may find comfort in listening to others talk about their experiences and learning how they have come out the other side, it may bring a source of comfort to them.

It's so hard to put into words how it actually feels to lose someone you love as there are no words that can define it, but the main thing to keep in mind is that there is no "normal" way to react.

Remember, this isn't the end, and life does go on.

For the purpose of this book, some identities and relationships have been changed.

For Mum

CHAPTER ONE

Motherless Mother

Grief Lesson # 1:
Remember The Journey.

It was July 2012 and I was in Worthing Hospital on the maternity ward, waiting for my mum to give birth to my youngest brother. I was half asleep, curled up inside the bathtub, feeling the cold tap dripping onto my feet. Half of me just couldn't be bothered to get up and tighten the tap while the other half was enjoying the relief from the cold drops of water, as it felt like I had been in a heatwave. The hospital room was scorching. It had been a long and exhausting night waiting for my brother to arrive, and Dad and I had been taking turns sleeping in the bathtub.

As I lay there, gradually waking up, I could hear Mum in the room next to me inhaling the gas and air and then squealing in pain seconds after. I shot out of the bath, almost slipping over on the floor from my drenched socks.

"Are you ready to meet your little brother?" the midwife asked, grinning at me.

I was only fourteen years old at the time but I kind of knew what to expect since I had regularly been watching the popular television series "One Born Every Minute" with Mum during her pregnancy.

My dad was on Mum's left side with one of his hands holding her hand and his other pinning her leg up, chanting "C'mon Sandra, come on. PUSH PUSH PUSH!" If you were standing outside that room not knowing what was going on, you would have thought my dad was watching the football with all the cheering he was doing.

Whilst my dad cheered my mum on, I was down at the bottom of the bed, sitting near the midwife and getting ready to take pictures, capturing the moment my little brother entered the world.

I remember feeling nervous, fidgeting on the spot whilst I stood at the bottom of the bed questioning every little thing that I caught sight of right in front of my eyes.

"Oh, what's that?"

"Is that normal?"

"Should that be so big?" – I had mistaken her placenta for another body part – I really thought her intestines or something had fallen out! Yes, laugh all you want readers!

It was hard to watch my mum be in such excruciating pain, clenching the bed sheets as she tried to find something to grab onto. It pretty much scarred me and put me off wanting to have kids myself. The excitement and the thrill of watching a baby be birthed was absolutely fascinating, yet scary. Whilst capturing every moment of my brother

—

being born, I was sobbing on the other end of the camera, relieved that Mum's horrifying howls were over. It was a very intense moment.

Seconds later this adorable, delicate baby had entered the world, screaming his tiny little lungs out with his first cry. My hands were quivering from having witnessed the most intense moment of my life, and my eyes were streaming with tears of joy. I had never felt so proud of Mum before this day. I immediately went up to her, gave her a kiss and a cuddle and told her just how proud I was of her, as Dad and the midwives gathered round, showering her with praise. "You did amazing Mum, I can't believe you just pushed out a baby!" I said, feeling amazed, as if I had just seen a party trick.

Mum was kissing my little brother's head as she deeply breathed in and out, trying to catch her breath.

It's such a surreal moment witnessing someone you love and care for do such a painful but rewarding thing as birthing a human. The whole time Mum was in labour and giving birth felt so powerful, and I was observing absolutely everything around me. When I looked between Mum and Dad, the tears were streaming freely. Dad isn't usually an emotional person, but his tears were unstoppable that day. The midwives were inspiring and interesting to witness – so calm yet demanding, guiding my mum with breathing techniques whilst she puffed on the gas and air like there was no tomorrow. Little did I know that five years later, Mum would be coaching me through the birth of my first child. Although it was a bit of a blur for me, I am so grateful that I had this moment captured for me too.

I will forever be grateful for having my mum around when my first child was born, because without her teaching me the ways of motherhood and guiding me through this new adventure, I wouldn't have had a clue on what clothes to buy or what baby products I needed, or her thoughts and opinions on what type of baby crib to get or even how to actually parent; it all meant so much to me. I knew how to take care of a child as I had worked with children from a young age and had helped my mum take care of my youngest brother, but I didn't know exactly how to actually be a mother. Taking care of children of your own is quite different to caring for someone else's child for a few hours. The amount of energy and time that goes into raising a child is exhausting but so rewarding.

My relationship with Mum was so special and unique. Of course, we would have times when we'd want to strangle each other, but what mother–daughter relationship isn't like that? She wasn't just a mother to me but she was also like a best friend and a sister all in one. She would be the first person I would call for anything, whether it were with good news, bad news or if I was genuinely bored.

I remember the exact moment I found out I was pregnant. It was a Saturday afternoon; the sun was shining and beaming through the windows. I was casually on the phone to my mum and I had randomly told her that I hadn't had my period yet. I remember having such a weird feeling in my stomach, like a knot. I was biting the insides of my cheeks, nervous to tell my mum as I didn't know how she was going to react. At the time I had only been with my partner Dominic for six months so I was beyond anxious.

"Go take a test, it won't do any harm to find out," she suggested.

I asked her to stay on the phone with me whilst I took the test that would determine my future.

The waiting game when you're watching for that second blue line to pop up is such an anxious time, it's almost like you can literally hear the ticking sound of a clock echoing inside your ears. As soon as I had taken the test, I looked the other way, placed this gross pee stick on the side of the sink and walked out of the bathroom. I continuously paced up and down in the bedroom, waiting for Mum to give me the go ahead to go back and check. "It's time, you can go check now," she said, and I could hear the nervousness in her voice as she grinned on FaceTime to me. When I went back to check the test, I screamed "Mum! There's another line!!" – "NO WAY!" my mum replied, ecstatically. We both screamed down the phone with excitement. I was in utter shock and my mum was so supportive, it was amazing.

I was so glad to have my mum's support because unfortunately when I announced to my "once" best friend hours later that I was indeed pregnant, she replied with, "OH MY GOD CHLOE!! You're not keeping It are you?!" which was a right kick in the teeth. So yes, I am very grateful to have had my amazing mother by my side through it all.

She came with me to my early scan when I was five weeks pregnant. I remember sitting in the waiting room swallowing the excessive amounts of water that my mum advised me to drink. "You need a full bladder so they can see bubba," she said. I couldn't stop fidgeting and worrying, and I'd often say to Mum, "What if there's no heartbeat and there's something wrong?" and she'd reply back with, "Whatever happens, I'm here. We will do this together."

Mum took me baby shopping and completely spoiled my daughter with clothes, toys, furniture. She even planned a surprise baby shower which was so thoughtful. I loved how excited she was – she downloaded the baby app so she could keep up to date with how big the baby was getting, sending me text messages of screenshots from the app explaining the size of the baby compared to all the fruits and vegetables. She was with me every step of the way. I loved watching her getting so excited over the fact that we'd be having a little bundle of joy soon; she'd boast about how she was going to be a nanny to all of her friends. Mum was such a social person and she'd talk to anyone, so when we were out shopping together and went to pay, she would speak to the cashiers and brag about how she still couldn't believe that her baby was having a baby, how she couldn't wait for the baby to arrive and how her granddaughter was going to be "a spoilt little munchkin".

I remember when I was around 35 weeks pregnant and I stayed at my parents' house to have some girly time with Mum; we did a homemade baby bump casting and Mum helped to slab the wet cast wraps onto my stomach. We were halfway through and the cast was awfully tight on my belly, and I started to get pains with hot flushes of heat – at that moment, I honestly thought I was going into labour. I felt claustrophobic, like the bathroom walls were closing in on me. I told Mum to help get the cast off – at that point it was rock hard and stuck to my stomach like a suction cup – whilst we were both laughing hysterically at the prospect of going into labour from a belly casting! Mum called the midwives and was advised to run me a bath, but by the time she was done on the phone and the bath had finished running, the pains had vanished.

I eventually went into labour at 39 weeks pregnant after being induced for two long days. It was the middle of the night and I was sitting on the birthing ball, absolutely drained and exhausted. My mum was sitting behind me and my partner was in front of me, both supporting me physically so I wouldn't fall to the floor. I was in so much pain and was passing out every five minutes from all of the awful contractions I was getting. I'd hear my mum's soothing voice drifting in the background saying "you can do this darling, it will all be over with soon" whilst she comforted me with a back rub. I heard her tell my partner how great he was doing with supporting me and remaining calm whilst I was screaming at the top of my lungs.

The midwife I had in the early hours of labour wasn't the best and she didn't support me that well, trying to persuade me to go onto the drip because I wasn't progressing quickly enough for her liking. The oxytocin drip is a drip that goes into a vein on your wrist/arm, and makes your contractions stronger than usual. The reason why I or other mothers may be against this method is because the pain that comes with getting the drip can make your labour more intense and painful. I had already been induced so the labour was intense enough and if I had gotten the drip it may have resulted in me getting an epidural which I really didn't want – needles are my biggest fear so God knows how I would have coped if I had to get one of those.

My mum wasn't happy with the way the midwife was trying to persuade me into getting the drip because she knew what birth I wanted. Thankfully the practitioner swapped with someone else for the night shift. Luckily the new lady was lovely and supportive – she even bopped along to the tunes we had blasting in the background whilst I pushed my daughter out.

During my pregnancy I had told my mum not to let me have an epidural because I was hoping to have a water birth; when I begged for an epidural whilst in labour Mum stood her ground and persuaded me not to have one. She'd say, "You can do this babe, just breathe through them with me, you are so strong darling." She was so natural at being a birthing partner, her soothing voice eased me and made me feel relaxed. Something about my mum being present whilst I was in labour and giving birth made me feel protected, like there was nothing to worry about. It meant so much to me to have her there as it was such an important moment in my life. My dad also joined in when I was about to give birth. I just vaguely remember that he casually entered the room with a McDonald's in his hand – a McDonald's that never got eaten by the way, instead my dad became the cameraman and filmed my labour.

I understand that not everyone has the privilege of having such a close relationship with their mums, having their mothers support them throughout their pregnancies or even having a mother at all, so I appreciated and cherished every moment I had with mine. I think many will agree that being a motherless mother is so bloody hard.

Grief Lesson # 2:
New journeys without that
person are difficult, but you are
allowed to have them.

I never knew how much I needed my mum until I found out I was pregnant with my second child. When I took the test this time round, it just wasn't the same feeling as I had experienced in that moment with my first. Taking this test all on my own, silently, made me feel odd, like I was missing a part.

I did the test on a Saturday around 6am. I had a gut feeling it was positive and after a few minutes had gone by, the ClearBlue timer finished loading and came up saying "pregnant". I smiled instantly but that spark soon went out when I realised that I couldn't tell Mum, that I couldn't call her to share this amazing news. I walked into the bedroom where Dominic was sleeping. He opened his eyes ever so slightly as I went to get into bed. "The test is positive, I'm pregnant," I whispered. "Are you?" he whispered back in a rough husky voice. His facial expressions didn't show much excitement at the news I had just announced to him, whether it was just him being sleepy or it was a typical man response, but I think I had just expected the same reaction from him that my mum would have given me. When I got back into bed, he patted my back as if to say, "well done". My brain spiralled a little bit as I lay there wide-eyed, thinking, "I don't know if I can do this, not without Mum."

I felt so blessed, but I still had this numb, sad feeling at the back of my head that would often stop me from being happy, making it that little bit harder to be excited about this pregnancy. Part of me was thrilled because I'd think of this pregnancy as a gift from Mum, but then another part of me wasn't, because I knew I had to do this alone without her, and although I had Dominic and the rest of my family there for me, I still felt alone through it all. It's just not the same as having your own mum to guide you through this amazing adventure together. It felt like I was a new mum all over again and everything I had learnt from my mum through my first pregnancy had been wiped from my memories.

Another reason why this pregnancy was so lonely was because I had to attend all of my scan appointments and hospital visits on my own. COVID had stopped all of us pregnant women from having our partners and family with us by our sides for support, making what should be our special pregnancy journey less exciting and more isolated.

Throughout my pregnancy I had so many questions that I wished I could have asked my mum; I would often picture in my head what she'd say or the way she would react to things and that would keep me focused sometimes. Baby shopping was hard and I tried to do most of it online, but I wasn't sure what items to buy or how many of each item of clothing I needed. I couldn't remember what to include when packing my hospital bag. I'd go baby shopping with my partner's sisters and although I enjoyed it, it still wasn't the same as having my mum's opinion and support. I often had to rely on mother and baby groups for answers to questions because I'd feel like a burden asking anyone I knew. I think I also felt slightly petty when it came to asking for advice because I didn't want to let anyone else in, I only wanted my mum to help me, which obviously wasn't possible.

A week after I found out I was expecting again, I did get in touch with one of my old friends who was expecting her first baby and was a week and a half ahead of me. We spoke near enough every day throughout our whole pregnancies and suddenly, I felt like the spark had been relit and I was actually able to feel excited about this amazing little baby. Speaking to someone who was pregnant at the same time really helped, like massively. As soon as I felt this pregnancy become hard and daunting, she swooped in at the perfect time. I don't think she knows just how thankful I am for her being there with me through my pregnancy journey whilst I was also grieving for the loss of Mum. Every day when we spoke we would compare our bumps – I was a huge hippo whilst she had a cute petite bump. We'd both count down the days until one of our scan appointments came up and then eventually our due dates.

One day I had an appointment at a private scan centre called Window to the Womb so I could see our baby boy when I was 29 weeks. My dad came with me to see him, and my friend had her scan to see her little boy at the same time, and it was nice to see another face whilst we were all in lockdown. Nobody tells you how lonely it can be during pregnancy, and being a mum in general – you're sitting there, day in and day out, doing the same routine, looking at the same four walls, going stir crazy. And with COVID mixed in, it just made it a lot more of a struggle, especially during the lockdowns, when we weren't allowed to see friends and family, and I had to stay at home with my own thoughts suffocating me.

When I was around 32 weeks pregnant, I attended an appointment with my midwife. The obstetrician and I were speaking about my birth plan, though there wasn't much to discuss except that I wanted to have a water birth and I only wanted gas and air for when I pushed. We started talking about how time had flown by and the midwife asked if we had everything ready and prepared for the big day.

"I bet your mother is so excited to have another little grandchild soon, will she be at your birth?" she asked me in her sweet, calming voice.

I had such a good relationship with my midwife – I would always feel so excited to go and see her. I don't know whether it was because during this pandemic it was just nice to see another face, or if it was me trying to leech onto someone who was like a mum figure. But as that dreaded question drifted out of her mouth, my stomach curdled, my eyes felt heavy and my heart sank. Whenever someone speaks about Mum, not knowing that she is in fact not alive anymore, it feels like being hit around the head with a shovel. Just a big smack in the face really. I knew this was coming at some point, but I had tried my best throughout my pregnancy to avoid speaking about Mum with any health professionals because I don't like explaining and repeating to everyone where my mum is and how she died. I'm not good with accepting any empathy at all as I get all awkward and stiff when I hear the words, "Oh no, I'm so sorry." The room goes all quiet and then you're just sat there, looking awkwardly around the room, thinking, "Well great, now she feels bad for asking" and then you start to feel bad for even mentioning it.

That wasn't the first time this question had been asked; the actual first time had felt even more uncomfortable. I attended a job interview three months after Mum died. Because life does go on and I needed money to pay bills. I was nervous, so nervous I hardly slept the night before. I felt sick to my stomach. The last time I had this feeling was my first day at secondary school. I nearly pulled out of going to the interview, but I could hear my mum's voice in the back of my head saying, "You can do this Chlo." And my dad took me to my interview which was another boost of support.

As I sat in this tiny, warm room, twiddling my thumbs, waiting for the manager to come and start the interview, I was nervous. And when I say I was nervous, I mean the type of nervous that had my hands clammy and sweaty like a dog had drooled all over them. I kept wiping them on my smart black flared trousers, eventually making them damp.

I had responded to all the interview questions when suddenly the manager asked: "What was the reason for you leaving your last job?", looking me dead in the eyes.

"Um, my mum died and was found just round the corner from where I worked, so I had to leave unfortunately, I didn't want to be reminded of her death every time I went there," I replied.

I remember scratching the skin on my hand as I said this to release some sort of pain whilst I had to speak about this event all over again. The manager relaxed her serious face and did a hard blink. "Oh god, I'm so sorry for your loss, that must have been awful for you," she replied in a sympathetic tone.

All you can say back to people who are showing empathy is "it's okay" or "it's fine".

Needless to say, I got the job but decided not to accept it in the end. I felt like the manager had only offered me the job because she felt sorry for me – whether this was the case or not, I'll never know. I just wish I didn't have to keep explaining to everyone where my mum is, I just wish that society wouldn't assume that everyone has a mum. Sometimes I wonder whether it would be easier to have a large badge clipped onto my shirt saying "Motherless" – that way, everyone would be able to see that I have no mum without me having to explain.

With my second pregnancy, I didn't allow myself to have a baby shower as this time round it just didn't feel right to be celebrating this baby without my mum being there. She planned my first baby shower with my partner's sisters which was such a lovely surprise – inviting my family and the friends I still had to celebrate my little girl. Instead of celebrating this baby with a shower, my partner's sisters planned a little meal out with me and my partner to shower us with gifts, which was really thoughtful of them.

When I was in labour with my second child, it was very straightforward, a thousand times better than my first. I had spontaneously gone into labour at 41 weeks and three days after a third sweep. I started getting pains around seven in the morning, and went to hospital at 11am. A few hours later I was in the pool getting ready to meet my little boy. I remember screaming for Mum whilst biting down and gulping on the gas and air, clutching onto Dominic's hand, digging my nails into his skin. I'd occasionally look around for a sign that Mum was present, as I'd always envisioned her showing some sort of sign that she was there supporting me. But obviously, it didn't happen. I was silly to think that it would be possible – that'll teach me to read spiritual stuff on Google.

I gave birth to our little boy at 2:19pm. It was such a beautiful moment, and once again, my partner, who never shows much emotion, let out a few tears on his arrival. Days later, I was feeling extremely vulnerable, the baby blues were hitting hard. When I'd get the chance to have a shower, I'd let out all my emotions and cry. I so desperately wanted my mum to be here with me, to help me. The grief I felt for my mum would overwhelm me at times and all I wanted to do was to ring her and hear her voice, reassuring me that the sleepless nights would get easier.

One time I reached for my phone in the middle of the night when I was awake feeding our baby. I pulled up her name in my contacts and stared at her number, knowing I couldn't speak to her, to beg her to come round and help me. I wanted to feel her tight cuddles and warm kisses on my forehead telling me that I was doing a great job. Despite being a young woman and a mum already, I still wanted to feel mothered. I will always feel a deep loss knowing my mum won't get to watch my daughter grow up or even meet her grandson, and that will always play on my mind.

My son's middle name is "Zander" in memory of my mum.

Both of the names Zander and Sandra are Greek and have the same meaning which is "defender of all people".

This saying couldn't be any truer as my mum defended and protected everyone she loved and cared for, and this was one of the many reasons why everyone loved her.

CHAPTER TWO

My Mum

Grief Lesson # 3:
Remember the loved one's you've
lost on the way.

Throughout the 22 years of life I had with Mum, she taught me more about life than any book ever could. One thing throughout my teen years that stands out was how she'd pound into my head to never be a doormat, constantly reminding me to stand up for myself. She wanted to prepare me for when I'd eventually find a partner. She'd say, "You are worth so much more, never let them take you for granted."

I remember when I had my first ever relationship. I was about fourteen years old, and the relationship lasted about a year. My first EVER heartbreak. Looking back, it makes me laugh so hard, like, bless my young little heart getting broken for the first time, thinking that this was what heartbreak felt like.

I had never felt heartbreak properly until Mum died.

As a teenager, I wouldn't let Mum through my locked door of emotions. I was a typical teen, hiding away in my bedroom, crying under the duvet covers, watching sad chick flick movies on TV. I remember Mum softly knocked on my door, peering her head round. "Are you okay? Do you want a cuddle?" she asked. I recall ever so slightly looking at her whilst hiding my face under the covers, trying to disguise my crying. "Oh come here," she said, almost welling up herself. She sat on my bed and cradled me like I was her little baby again. She tried to comfort me by telling me stories of when she had her first heartbreak with Dad, reassuring me that I wasn't alone and that everyone experiences a heartbreak at least once in their lives.

When I would get upset, Mum would try to make me feel better by telling silly jokes, trying to pin me down and tickle me till it hurt and showering me with comfort food, hugs and kisses. Thinking back, at the time I almost felt silly being in my mum's arms whilst crying, but as I got older I appreciated her cradled hugs more and more. It wasn't until she was gone that I realised how much I craved those precious hugs; the closest I will get to hugging her now is when I picture and imagine her in my mind.

When I'd have arguments with my partner Dominic, I'd go and have sleepovers with Mum, just like some people do with a best friend. And Mum was literally like a best friend to me as well as a mother. She would listen to me rage and rant about my feelings, crying it all out. No matter what, she would reassure me that everything would sort itself out in the end and that, "If it's meant to be, it'll be". She'd remind me that her and my dad had these little tiffs too when she was my age, but in the end, they always found each other again.

Mum met Dad in 1996, when she was seventeen years old and working in a nursing home. Dad was a chef at the nursing home and Mum was a care assistant, caring for all the elderly residents. They had hit it off after Dad invited Mum out for some drinks. They had been together since May the second, Mum's birthday. They were together for 23 years in total, married for eleven. Throughout those 23 years of being together they had their ups and downs, just like all couples do. But they always pulled through.

Whilst I was growing up, Mum always taught me and my brother that money doesn't grow on trees, although I'd sarcastically reply to her comment and say, "Well actually, it's made out of paper so technically it does" and then she'd give me the biggest death stare, basically telling me to shut the F-up, haha! I think I was about eleven or twelve years old when I started doing little jobs for my parents to earn money for things I wanted to buy myself. For example, cleaning the house – and when I say cleaning the house, I don't mean just a quick polish and hoover, it was an intense deep clean. Mum would write me the biggest list ever of all the things that needed doing in the house, and I would do this over two days. The list would contain chores like bleaching bathrooms, cleaning out the kitchen cupboards, hoovering and steaming the floors, re-organising toy boxes, de-weeding the garden. The whole shebang. My parents taught me simple life skills – Mum taught me how to keep a home running and Dad taught me (and continues to teach me) how to cook. And I can't thank them enough for making me learn these basic things. If I hadn't learnt all of this as a child I probably wouldn't have a scooby on how to do any of these things in my own home now.

Mum was so supportive when my best friend Katie died from cancer back in 2017. I will never forget the moment and how I felt when I found out the news of her passing. I had woken up around four or five in the morning because I was due to travel with Dominic and his family up to Hull for his sister's university graduation. As I sat on the end of the bed sipping my cup of tea, I grabbed my phone to read the digital newspaper (aka social media) and I straightaway noticed the message on my screen from my friends group chat suggesting that we all needed to meet to have a drink in memory of Katie. I came off the chat and went straight onto Facebook. My heart was pounding away in my chest like a boxer going at it with the speed ball. As I saw her family's announcement, I dropped to the floor feeling lifeless, sobbing my heart out.

I hadn't met up with Katie in about a year due to me being pregnant, and then having a new-born and adjusting to being a new mum. Six months prior to becoming pregnant I had just got together with my partner and we all know that at the beginning of a relationship it's all lovey dovey and you're both absorbed in the honeymoon period. Life does get in the way sometimes. But you see, we had that type of friendship, the type where if we were to meet after a long time it wouldn't be awkward, not at all. The type of friendship that had a connection so strong that time and distance couldn't corrode it.

For example, before Katie had gotten ill and I fell pregnant, I think the longest time we had gone without seeing each other was about a month. One evening, my partner went on a night out with the lads while Katie and I had gone to the pub. She'd asked curiously how it felt being with my partner, the guy who was the popular one at school. We gossiped and laughed all night and our friendship was just the way it always had been.

I think a big factor in my pain from her loss was regret: I regretted not reaching out to her and meeting up before it was too late – it devastated me that I never got to say goodbye. I was absolutely gutted. We would make plans to meet but then she'd get too sick or something would come up at my end; life speeds up way too quickly all of a sudden, like someone's just pressed the fast forward button on a TV remote. I think none of us realise that we need to grab the moment until something like the demise of a loved one occurs.

My mum came with me to Katie's funeral and wake, not just to support me but because she wanted to pay her respects too. I remember grabbing my mum's hand and squeezing it tight as Katie's coffin was carried down the aisle. I broke down in tears and felt my heart breaking away bit by bit.

Grieving for a friend is quite different to grieving for a parent or even a pet. I grieved in different ways with each loss.

With Quest, our springer spaniel dog, it was literally like losing a family member. Of course, we all knew this day was going to come at some point so we had time to prepare ourselves, but it was still so sad, she was such a bundle of joy and I loved seeing her little face every day. I remember when she was a pup and she'd always sit and snuggle up in my lap to go to sleep; as she grew bigger, she would still try to sit in my lap even though she could hardly fit there. Grieving for Quest was painful at the beginning, it took about a month for the intensity to settle and then I started to feel less pain as time went on.

With Katie, it was a real shock finding out the news of her passing. It took about a year and a half for the sadness to pass. I'd sit there most days regretting and hating myself for not meeting up with her before she died, there were so many things that I wished I could have spoken to her about. But you do learn to deal with the pain, and over time that pain gets easier, and you accept what happened. It's been about four years now and when I think about Katie, I don't get that empty sad feeling anymore, instead I think about all the happy memories that we were able to share. Of course, I'll always miss her but I'm not grieving with pain anymore.

Now, with Mum it's a totally different pain. Not only was it so sudden and tragic, but she was my mother. Losing a parent is to lose the person who raised you up and taught you the ways of life; the person who made all those special memories with you as a child; who worked so hard to give you everything you needed and wanted in life. The person who'd protect you and would do anything for you. The person who would call you every single day without fail, making sure you were okay. Suddenly, they are gone. Vanished. Capoof.

One day Mum was here, the next she was gone. And I think to myself, if she had died of natural causes, then maybe, just maybe, I would be grieving differently. Maybe the grief wouldn't be so intense, so excruciatingly painful both mentally and physically.

As children, we don't think of our parents as a whole person. We know that they have jobs, maybe they have one or two friends, but we see them only through the narrow lens of a child.

Grief Lesson # 4:
Grief is a lonely world, but it
doesn't have to be.

After losing my mum, I realised that people other than myself and my family were experiencing a loss too. Grief makes you feel alone and isolated. But it doesn't have to if you remember that others have lost someone too.

Mum worked as an area manager for a care home; she was a dedicated, hardworking woman. Back when I was still living with my parents, Mum would usually come home at around 5 or 6pm. Me, my dad and brothers would be eating dinner at the dinner table and when I'd hear the front door unlock, my chest would feel like it was glowing up, knowing that Mum was finally home. I was like a little puppy that would get over excited with their owner. Mum would go upstairs to her room and jump straight into her pj's, have dinner and sit in her bed working from her laptop till about 9pm, maybe later. Sometimes she'd get the odd work call if she was on-call and would have to go back in and help, then she wouldn't come home till possibly the early hours of the morning. It took her many years to work her way up to where she wanted to be. She started working in a nursing home when she was seventeen to gain experience in care.

After she had me and I turned four years old, she started working in a care home, slowly working her way up to manager, then area manager.

"If tears could build a stairway and memories a lane, I'd walk up to Heaven and bring you home again." – Karen White

Below are some favourite memories that some of my mum's work colleagues, best friends and our family have told me of. I remember Mum coming home from work sometimes and she would be in hysterics telling us about some of these.

What are your most favourite memories of Mum?

Work colleague and friend: "Me and Andy wrapped her in cling film to the chair at work!"

Work colleague and friend: "There are so many. When Sandra came over to my home and took the absolute piss out of me and said I was having a massive baby with my baby bump looking so big – I did the same with her when she was pregnant with your brother. There were so many laughs trying to do a restraint on the children at work and the kids would cover themselves in soap and oil so we couldn't pin them down as they were so slippery, and we would laugh so much it hurt. Your mum was so over tired from the night shift but would still be up early in the morning to wash and dry her hair ready for the day ahead."

Friend: "This is a tough one as I have so many memories of us growing up together since we met at the age of nine... She was and always will be the first ever best friend I had. Always there for me during some tough times even though she was more often than not dealing with her own personal issues. She would always put others before herself. She had one of the biggest hearts ever."

Support teacher: "Coming into the school and taking you out of the isolation room saying you're not staying haha!"

Cousin: "When we were kids and she came to stay with us for a bit when we lived in Southampton. We went out exploring the woods near where we lived."

Cousin: "I remember on the day of her wedding, going to your house with Mum and seeing her all ready in her dress, she looked amazing."

Cousin: "When we were still at school, she was on the local news... they had been taught swear words at school and her mum went mad and called the local newspaper, and it was on the local news one evening."

Colleague and friend: "We were pregnant at the same time, her with your brother and me with the twins!"

Colleague and friend: "I also remember another time when she picked me up from mine to go on our works Christmas do. We were driving along the A27 towards the Southwick tunnel in the right hand lane (in her red Micra) and this car came right up behind us trying to get us to move to the left but she was like 'Sod him! I'm staying here now!!' The guy was flashing us but she was just laughing! She always stood her ground."

Stepmother: "My favourites would be the times we would meet up for coffee and catch ups, those were special moments."

Friend: "Very kind and thoughtful lady. I remember your mum coming to our house when Katie passed away."

Friend: "We shared a love of all things Disney! She was a fantastic Mum."

Neighbour: "I used to love the conversations we had, either standing in the garden talking over the fence or standing outside our front doors, they would last for hours."

Colleague and friend: "When she was so proud to bring you on a work night out. And staying late for hours preparing for Ofsted, such a boring task if it wasn't for doing it with fun people." – I remember this night out, I went clubbing with her and her work friends and I remember how people in the streets assumed we were sisters because we looked so alike, and I think this was because my mum appeared so young too. She was always so pleased to show me off and I loved introducing my mum to my friends too, because she was such a funny person and had a very outgoing personality, anyone could get on with her like a house on fire.

Colleague and friend: "I was about to be attacked by a young lad with a lump of wood. Just as I was expecting the first blow to land, Sandra leapt out of nowhere and pinned the lad to the floor. Weirdly something we used to laugh about years after."

Colleague and friend: "Loved our supervisions, which although highly professional would descend into chaos and laughter."

Colleague and friend: "She always had my back! Honestly, that's all I can remember… we just laughed a lot."

Friend: "She reached out to me many times when she knew that I had lost my little boy. He was a sleeping baby. She kept checking in on me."

I miss the times when I'd go up to Mum's home office and wait for her to finish getting ready, she'd take for-everrrr. Putting her makeup on, drying her hair, then straightening it. But now, I'd happily turn back time and sit there, admiring her reflection in the mirror.

These are just some of the memories I was told, and it just shows how much of an impact Mum's bubbly-self had on everyone. You are idolised by many, Mum.

CHAPTER THREE

Halloween Night

Grief Lesson # 5:
Never expect every day to be the
same.

It was 5pm on October the 31st – Halloween night. I'd just finished taking some photos of my daughter in her spooky "Annabelle" Halloween costume, and had lit my cinnamon spice candle. We were ready to sit down in the lounge and carve our pumpkins together with "Casper the Ghost" on TV in the background.

After finishing off our first pumpkins, I thought to myself "Ah, Mum's probably home now, I'll give her a call." I tried to FaceTime her to show her our carved pumpkins. I was going to suggest that me and my daughter go round and spend the evening at her house as my partner was working his night shift, but she didn't pick up. At that moment, I didn't think anything of her not answering my call as she'd normally call back shortly after.

A couple of minutes later, I received a text from Mum which said, "Babe I've just pulled up home and going indoors. I will call you later when I'm sorted xxxx" Oddly, she didn't call back later that evening when she was "sorted", so I assumed she had gone to bed. Mum would sometimes go to bed early if she'd had a long day at work.

Dad told me a couple of days later that when Mum had arrived home, she'd gone up into her make-up room to get ready. Dad described to me how she was all dressed in black and sitting down at her vanity desk, fixing her make-up. "You're not going out again are you?" he had asked her, feeling disappointed. Mum wouldn't normally miss Halloween night – or any occasion for that matter. She would usually stay home and watch Halloween films or go out trick or treating with my youngest brother. Mum and Dad weren't in the best of places in their relationship at this point, so he assumed she was just going out to leave some space between them. "I'm going to see a friend; I'll be back later," she had replied bluntly.

The next day, November the 1st, it was around seven in the morning and I was still asleep in bed and my phone started ringing. I ignored the call as I was still half asleep and my phone was on the cabinet halfway across the room. It then rang again, so I assumed it was my mum calling. I got up and checked my phone. I remember thinking "how odd" as I looked down and saw a missed call from my mum's friend. "What's up?" I messaged. "Can you send me your dad's number please, it's important," he replied.

I was curious. "What the hell is going on?" I remember saying out loud, whilst my partner and daughter were still sleeping in bed behind me. I messaged back saying, "I just called Chris and Mum isn't home, is she with you? What is she doing?" He instantly replied saying, "Chloe please, give my number to your dad, it's about your mum. She's not in a good place, she's not with me... I really need to speak with your dad." I called my dad straightaway and told him what my mum's friend had messaged me, and he immediately called said friend and told me that he'd update me with what was going on after he had spoken with him.

After talking to Dad and my mum's friend, I was left wondering and thinking all sorts of possible scenarios in my head. My partner woke up after hearing me on the phone with my dad. "What's going on?" he asked, sounding concerned and looking dazed. He had only had a few hours sleep that morning as he had returned home from his night shift a few hours ago. After I filled him in with the details, he tried reassuring me by saying, "I'm sure everything's fine." At one point I thought that maybe Mum had done a naughty and gone drinking and that she was just hungover at one of her friend's houses.

I waited for what felt like forever to hear back from my dad; he eventually FaceTimed me about fifteen minutes later. "She's taken pills, Chloe, I don't know what pills, but the police are trying to find her. God knows why she'd do this!" my dad furiously said to me, stuttering over his words and sounding distressed. I started welling up when he mentioned the word "pills".

"Don't say that!" I cried down the phone. "I'll be down in ten minutes," I told him. The moments after I put down the phone are a bit of a blur as I shot out of bed and got dressed as fast as I could. My mind had gone into a bit of a meltdown and it felt like wires in my brain were tying into thousands of knots as I worried about my mum more and more. I was rushing around the house whilst my partner tried to calm me down and said, "Don't think the worst, she's probably fine."

I got into my partner's car with him and my daughter, me in the passenger seat and my partner beside me driving. I felt agitated, restless. I was trying to stay calm and think more positive. "Everything is going to be okay," I kept repeating to myself in my head.

"Where do you think she is then? It's just so weird how nobody knows where she is," Dominic said to me. I remember having a short conversation with him. "I don't think anything bad has happened, like I think she's probably asleep somewhere, but the fact that Dad mentioned the word 'pills' has made me wonder," I replied. I was quite concerned as this was completely out of the blue and nobody knew where she was. The fact that the police were also out looking for her made things sound more alarming.

We arrived at my parents' house and I told Dominic I'd call him as soon as we knew where Mum was. "I'm sure we'll find her in a minute, she's probably at one of her friend's houses asleep knowing her," I said to him, not knowing what the hell I was about to walk into.

CHAPTER FOUR

We Never Said Goodbye

Grief Lesson # 6:
There is no way to prepare
yourself.

I walked into my parents' house and the first people I saw were two police officers. One of them was in the lounge speaking to my youngest brother who was seven at the time; she was trying to occupy him with his toys, asking him questions about his favourite army figure. The other police officer was in the kitchen with my dad. They were going through everything that had happened with Mum the night before and they were trying to listen out for any news. Mum's disappearance had me feeling anxious and I just stood there in the hallway listening to all the sounds in the background whilst watching Dad in a panic. The dog was barking at the police officers, while from the radios attached to their jackets I could hear their fellow police officers tuning in, muffling different words. My youngest brother walked around playing with the police lady, completely oblivious to what was going on.

My eldest brother came walking towards me and asked in a concerned tone, "Have you heard any news? I sent Mum a text last night asking if Lee could come round and she replied at 5am this morning."

"No, I haven't heard anything. It's so weird how she's just gone. I do think she's just sleeping at her friend's house though," I replied. I was just as confused as he was.

"Any news?" I asked my dad.

"No, they're still looking for her. They are trying to trace the last call she had with her friend to see if it gives them a location," he replied, frantically walking past me to head into the lounge.

I remember the worried look in his eyes. I had never seen my dad's face like that before. He loved my mum so much and I was so scared for him, because if anything had happened to her then I didn't know how he would cope.

The police radios continued to go off and my dad heard a little muffled voice on the radio saying that a dog walker had described seeing a woman with black hair in a red car, but Dad didn't think anything of it. "That isn't Sandra," he said in such disbelief. Seconds later, my dad walked up the stairs and one of the police officers followed behind him. I assumed they had gone upstairs to look for something to help the police find Mum.

The police lady came up to me and was asking what I do for a living, if I was close with my mum, if I have any children. She was just trying to distract me with a load of random questions, but looking back it was obvious that she was trying her hardest to divert my attention from the agony I was about to feel. A few minutes later we all heard this almighty thud on the wall coming from upstairs,

---

followed by a heart-wrenching scream from my dad. In that second, everything stopped, and time stood still.

As I'm writing this next part, I can still hear the sound of my dad's heart breaking, it's engraved forever in my head. It has truly traumatised me and I will never forget it. Whenever I think about that moment and re-run it through my mind, I can remember every little detail.

"SHE'S GONE!-NO!-NO-NO!" my dad screamed with horror.

Nobody had to announce the devastating, tragic news to me and my brothers. We already knew. I could hear the police officer saying to my dad, "Peter, Peter, calm down, I've got you." It sounded like he was trashing the whole of the upstairs, slamming his body to the ground, hitting the walls over and over again as he tried to let out his anger and pain.

It felt like my whole world had crashed down on me, like a huge piece of my heart had been ripped out of my body. I felt like I was having a panic attack. My breath came in short bursts as my heart hammered against my chest. The world seemed to spin as I fought to breathe, every breath was a struggle. It was the worst day of my life.

I kept repeating to myself in my head, "It's not real, this can't be real, surely she's not gone?!" as my body dropped down to the ground at the bottom of the stairs. The police officer came up to me and kneeled down.

"Are you okay? Is there anyone I can call for you for support?" she asked me.

"No...no... I just need to sit down for a second. Are my brothers okay?" I instantly asked, shoving my feelings aside.

My youngest brother was standing in the lounge, shaking his hands and fidgeting on the spot, looking directly at me with fear in his eyes as he listened to the horrifying screams coming from our dad. "What's wrong with Daddy?" he cried to me. "Where's Mummy?" he shouted.

"It's okay, everything's okay," I reassured him, wrapping my arms around him and holding him as tight as I could. The police officer took over from me and comforted my youngest brother so I could check on my eldest brother, Chris. He was sitting on the sofa with his hands over his eyes, tears rolling down his face. The last time I had seen my brother cry was when he was a little boy.

"Oh Chris, our mum," I cried, unable to finish what I had planned to say. As we both sat there together, my arms over his head, it felt like my brother's soul had just left his body as he leaned his heavy head upon my shoulder. All I could think about was the fact that I knew deep down, from this moment on, nothing would be okay. All of our lives had just been torn apart and thrown into a shredding machine.

Afterwards, I called my partner. I couldn't say the words to him, but he knew what had happened. "She's gone," I wailed down the phone. He immediately came to my parents' house to support me.

The house felt cold, empty and like a literal graveyard. I remember taking myself into the kitchen to sit down for a second, trying to process everything that I had just witnessed. The other police officer came into the kitchen to sit with me for support. I sat there at the table with a pale face, probably looking like I had just seen a ghost.

"I am so sorry for your loss, honestly. This must be so hard for you. Were you close with your mum?" he said to me in his most empathetic voice.

Grief Lesson # 7:
Don't ask questions until you are
prepared for the answers.

"It's okay... yes, I was very close with Mum, I just can't believe it, you know? How was she found?" I asked him, almost stuttering over my words.

The look on his face when I asked him that question was like I had just done something so disturbing he couldn't believe his eyes. But I just had to know.

If I'm honest, I wish I hadn't asked at all. He told me the details, which are now engraved into my brain. The little details he told me have given me nightmares ever since.

CHAPTER FIVE

Announcing The News

Grief Lesson # 8:
Allow yourself to depend on
others.

Moments after Dominic walked through the door, my eyes locked onto him like I was a leech. I walked over to him, buried my head into his chest and let out an enormous cry. He placed his hand over my head and whispered, "It's okay, cry as much as you need to."

I remember my body shaking from all of the shock, but I also felt some sort of relief, as I released these painful emotions I was feeling so deeply onto someone else. He was my safe haven, and he was so incredible with supporting me. I felt like I was safe when he was by my side throughout all the raw days.

The first week was a bit of a blur, and all I'm able to remember is what everyone around me was doing and how they were feeling. But I can't remember how I was coping. Dominic told me I wouldn't let him out of my sight, it was almost as if I was afraid that something bad might have happened if he had left my side.

Dominic took care of all of us; he stayed with me at my parents' house until I was ready to go back home, which was four months in total. He didn't have to stay with me, he could have gone back home and left me to it. But being the amazing man he is, he wanted to be with me, to comfort me and support me through all of it. Throughout our time together, I think that was the first time I had ever seen pain and worry in Dominic's eyes. I could see that he was worried about me, that he was hurting for me too.

It wasn't just me that he supported, he was also there for my dad too, lending a shoulder to cry on and, when Dad needed someone to talk to other than someone emotionally connected to the situation, Dominic was available. When Dad and I didn't eat due to the misery killing our appetite, Dominic bought us takeaways – he even bought a new gaming console (Oculus Quest) to cheer everyone up, which it did. It cheered us all up and we were able to crack a laugh out at times too. It was a good distraction for us on the gloomy, difficult days we were going through.

I'm so grateful for my partner, and although I may not show this enough sometimes, I hope he knows just how grateful I really am. He saw me on my worst, darkest days when I just sat there, crying, screaming and shouting; when I had nightmares about my mum, waking up in such distress. He willingly sat and listened to me talk about Mum – he's been with me through all of it. He later told me that it was one of the worst experiences of his life having to watch us all be in so much pain. Dominic described walking into our home as if he had walked into a horror show. We were all wailing with a deep, intense painful cry.

43

After I found out that Mum had died, it was all a bit of a blur due to the intense information I was trying to comprehend. I was in the lounge, sitting on the edge of the sofa, my body hunched with my head in the palm of my hands, puzzling on what to think or do next. Dad was sitting opposite me, and the police officer was crouched down next to him trying to comfort him, advising him to stay on the sofa as he could barely keep himself standing – he was in so much pain internally that he would crash to the floor. So the best place for him was the sofa.

His eyes were puffy and bloodshot from all the tears that were crashing down while he yelped, "Why did she have to leave us?! She's so silly. What are we going to do Chlo? How are we going to live?" I'll be honest with you all, I could just have said that I knew everything would be alright, like almost everyone around me was telling me, but I felt sick to my stomach. It felt like someone had reached inside my body, snatched my heart and soul out and chucked them down a deep dark well, making sure they were well out of my reach. I grabbed my dad's hand and held it tight whilst wiping my runny nose with my other hand.

"We'll get through this Dad," I said to him.

"I have nobody now, you have no mum and I have no wife. We are now all on our own!" Dad yelled.

"Oh Pete, don't be silly, I'll be here for you all won't I Chlo? Everything is going to be okay," my nan said in her most innocent voice, bless her heart.

I had suggested to Dad that we should inform Mum's side of the family.

"Fuck no, they don't deserve to know, they're probably the reason she took her life!" he screeched, spluttering from his mouth.

I had never seen my dad so bitterly angry in all my years of life, it was horrible and it shattered my heart to see him in this state of mind.

"Her brothers deserve to know, but you're right, her parents don't," I responded.

Dad agreed so I went and sat at Mum's desk, twiddling my thumbs whilst trying to mentally prepare myself before calling my uncle.

For ten minutes I was making up different scenarios in my head of how the conversation might go whilst on the phone to him. I was sobbing at the thought of calling – I could barely hold a conversation with anyone in the house without blubbering, let alone talking to someone over the phone. I finally called my uncle. No answer. I called again, still no answer. "Hi James, can you call me back ASAP," I messaged him. He replied almost immediately saying, "What's up?"

"It's to do with Mum, please call," I replied. I remember my hands were shaking awfully. Typing messages with weepy eyes and shaky hands is a task that I mastered that day.

I tried calling again as I felt that this news shouldn't come by something as impersonal as a text, but again no answer.

"Dad wants to speak to you, it's urgent," I messaged him after calling for the third time.

"I'm in the middle of a meeting, what's wrong?" he replied.

Honestly in that moment I thought to myself, "Damn it, just answer already." I really didn't want to break the news of Mum's death over text message, it was the last thing I wanted to do. But he wouldn't answer my calls so I just came out with it and messaged him: "Mum's dead."

My heart sank when I sent it – I can't begin to imagine how he must have felt when reading my response.

"What?" he replied bluntly.

"My mum's dead, call me when you can," I replied.

He obviously hadn't realised how serious things were – he must have thought that me messaging him was just a way of trying to lure him in so my mum could speak with him as they hadn't spoken for years. He clearly didn't realise how awful the reason for me messaging was. He rang me back straight away; I answered and instantly bawled my eyes out, intensely sobbing down the phone to him. He said he'd be right over with my mum's other brother, which gave me a sense of relief. The more family that came, the less alone I felt, and the less responsible for dealing with everything on my own.

My mother's side of the family was a bit all over the place, like missing puzzle pieces. She hadn't spoken to her brothers in years. She didn't speak to her parents either. But she had a step-mum and a step-brother and sister who treated her like a proper family and welcomed her with open arms.

A couple of hours later I had to call up my work to ask if I could have some time off to stay with my family to grieve. My boss was so understanding about it all as she too had lost someone in her life. "My gosh Chloe, I am so sorry to hear," she gasped. She was as shocked as I was when I first found out. She had met my mum a few times in the past when she had come to pick my daughter up from my work whilst I was stuck in meetings. I worked in the same nursery that my daughter went to.

Me and my boss had a little chat about how Mum died, when I found out, how me and my family were feeling, all the little details. And I was SO grateful that she had taken the time to listen and talk. "Take as much time as you need and remember, if you ever need to talk, please call me or come in and chat." It made me sob just that little bit more. It's kind of rare to have nice bosses nowadays. Since starting work at the age of fourteen, I haven't met a nicer boss than her. So, if you are reading this, thank you from the bottom of my heart.

As the hours went by, Dad and I thought it would be best to announce the news of Mum's passing via Facebook. I know some of you may be thinking "Why does she feel the need to announce on social media so soon?" We had so many friends on Facebook and we didn't have their numbers at the time, they were all in Mum's phone which was locked as she had changed her passcode that day. It was easier to announce it on there so everyone could see at once rather than messaging them all separately. And if I'm honest, I didn't want to be sitting for hours on end calling every one individually, telling them the same thing over and over again and then having to answer the same questions.

"Oh gosh, I'm so sorry for your loss, are you okay?" "What happened?" Like, no, I'm most definitely not okay and no, I will not be telling you right now the details of how my mother has died. I probably was a bit selfish in that sense, to not call everyone directly. Looking back, I didn't realise how the news of Mum's death would impact other people's feelings. All I could think about that day was how I felt and how my dad and brothers were feeling.

"To all our family and friends, this morning my beautiful mother Sandra Whyte passed away. We are all very broken and no words can explain how much pain we are all in, we will all miss her very dearly and I still can't get my head around it. I love you so much Mum, you were my best friend and I wish I could change things and change how you felt. We will all try and stay strong for you. Until we meet again."

The number of comments and messages that came flooding in was overwhelming. After I posted the announcement, I muted my notifications and stayed off my phone, because the more I read the messages and comments, the more it would become real, it was like rubbing salt in a wound.

About four days after Mum's passing, a few people suggested that we should set up a GoFundMe page to raise funds for her funeral. We wanted to give her the best send-off possible, so I set up the page and many generous people donated and shared. A day later, I received an email from a reporter who worked for the local newspaper. In the email he said, "I was thinking we might be able to help share the fundraiser through an article, which could be a tribute piece to Sandra celebrating her life as well as directing readers to the GoFundMe page to raise as much money as possible."

Seventh November, the day that Mum was in the newspaper, my dad, my cousin Lynsey and I all walked to the shop that was just down the road from Dad's house and bought a few of the newspapers to keep. Dad didn't go inside the shop because he knew her photo would be displayed on the counter. I went in with Lynsey and silently gasped as I caught a glimpse of Mum's photo on the front page of the newspaper that was laid out on the counter. I knew she'd be there as I was the one who had written the tribute, but it was still a shock to actually see it, at the time it was so surreal. When we walked out to go back home, I hugged the newspaper ever so tightly, I wouldn't let it out of my sight. I didn't read the paper and I still haven't read it because it hurts.

Dad walked home in tears, dragging the painful weight he was carrying with him. The best way to describe the way he walked was as if a chained weight were attached to his ankles – you know, the ones that the prisoners wear in comics to stop them from running away. Dad had his hands in his pockets the whole time, his head lowered slightly staring at the ground. He was there, but only physically.

Many big-hearted people helped us raise a total of £2,775 on the GoFundMe page. I can't put into words how grateful I am to everyone who helped us raise so much money for her funeral. Without that money, we wouldn't have been able to have given her the send-off that she truly deserved.

CHAPTER SIX

What If?

*Grief Lesson # 9:
Don't punish yourself over the
unknown.*

"If only she had just come to me to tell me how she felt."

"What if the police had found her sooner?"

"If only I had supported her better."

When you experience a suicide loss, you are forever questioning yourself, asking the "what ifs?", wondering what you could have done to prevent a loved one from taking their own life. You'll be sat there punishing yourself and making yourself believe that if only YOU had done better, then maybe they'd still be alive now.

Please remember that you are not to blame – don't ever punish yourself or think this is your fault. We aren't in control of or responsible for other people's actions because we just don't know what some people are capable of. Unless you are actually told, or you have a suspicion, then there is really no way to know.

When I talked with Dad about Mum we would speak about how both of us felt we could have helped her more. Dad would say, "I keep saying to myself, if only she had just come to me, I could have helped her. I always told her that she could speak to me about anything." I'd reply with, "I know, but you shouldn't blame yourself. I ask myself the same questions every day, like what if I had seen her more and asked how she was feeling lately. What if she had just gone to the doctors and told them about how she was feeling." We both beat ourselves up over the fact that we didn't notice the signs – looking back, it was so clear that she was acting out of character. But unfortunately, hindsight is 20-20, you only realise when it's too late and you're analysing everything in the past, every event that happened leading up to their death.

Sadly, the difficult truth is that neither of us were able to save her because we had no clue how she was feeling at the time, she had only opened up to one person. Maybe it was a cry for help and it resulted in Mum taking things too far, too far to fix.

I have learnt not to blame myself anymore – it was damaging my mental health because every day I would beat myself up and tell myself that I could have helped her, that I was stupid for not noticing that my own mother was suffering. But I also thought about what if she had been saved. How long would it have been until she had tried to do this again? Weeks? Months? Would she have gotten better, felt better? It's something that we will never find out.

When someone takes their own life, usually they don't do it because of just one problem. It's normally a build-up of events that have happened to them in the past. In Mum's case, she had faced many events and situations throughout her life that had caused her to feel this way. Everything had sadly gotten too much for her, these problems had suffocated her and eventually made her feel like she was not good enough, so worthless that she felt that the only way out was to end her life.

From when I was a young girl, Mum had told me many stories from her past, situations that had left her feeling worthless, sad and depressed. Mum was very open when she told me about her bad relationship with her parents – she didn't get along with them at all when she was young and had ended up moving out of her mother's house when she was 17. Before Mum and Dad got pregnant with me, she had unfortunately experienced a miscarriage whilst on a nine-hour flight home from her first holiday to Florida with my dad and her brother.

When she gave birth to me, she sadly experienced post-natal depression. Mum told me that at times when she was recovering from giving birth to me, her mother would come round and make her do the cleaning and ironing and sometimes would throw a little dig in about her parenting. It almost sounded like the story about Cinderella who couldn't go to the ball and instead had to clean her step-mother's house. But in Mum's case, she couldn't have her beloved baby until she cleaned up her own home and did the tasks her mother had given her.

When I was about eight years old and my brother was four, Mum found out that a couple of family friends had betrayed her trust and had been abusing both myself and my brother when we were under their care whilst Mum and

Dad were working. This was really hard to tell our parents and when we did mention it to them, it affected Mum badly. She was livid and felt like she couldn't trust anyone. Throughout Mum's life there were many people who abused her trust and made her feel worthless. A HUGE factor as to why Mum felt so sad and would get really down at times was because her side of the family wouldn't speak to her. Fortunately, she had a step-mother, brother and sister who treated her like any family should treat one another.

A few years ago, my brother had become depressed. My mum found out and it was a very upsetting time for us all. We were all really cautious and made sure that we were doing everything we could to make him feel better than he was. As a mother, you try to do your absolute best to make your child feel loved and to protect them from this cruel world. My mum never spoke about how she felt when my brother was depressed – to be honest, she was a very closed book about her emotions and would always hide behind her smile.

But it was so much more than Mum's childhood – mental health is a complicated thing, and there are only so many blows a person can take. Work was hard for Mum at times and being an area manager must have been even more stressful with all the responsibility – even on weekends, Mum would be doing work stuff, she never stopped unless we were away on an actual holiday. Mum worked with children and she was very passionate about her job. She told me about the time when a colleague she worked with was being horrible to her, especially name calling. On a few occasions, I witnessed her come home and break down in tears to my dad, and it's sad, really really sad. People need to learn to be kind and to take responsibility for their actions. Words that mean nothing to one person can tear another apart. It's not hard to be nice.

In October, one month before Mum died, she started speaking to a friend who was depressed. This was when Mum started acting out of character. I always ask myself, "If she had never spoken to her friend, would she still be here now?" I don't know if it was a coincidence that her mental health deteriorated so quickly the minute she started speaking to her friend, but I will always wonder.

Mum always put her emotions on the backburner for the ones she loved and I wonder how that must have affected her too.

Throughout the years before she left us, there had been so many uplifting moments. In 2018, we all went to Florida in America for three weeks so Mum and Dad could renew their vows. And in February 2019, Mum bought the dog of her dreams – she had wanted a pug for so long and she had begged my dad every day and, as always, he eventually gave in and welcomed Milly the pug into our family home.

In August (three months prior to her death), Mum, Dad and my brothers all went to Cornwall for a week and they had also taken my daughter too. Mum FaceTimed me every day and sent me photos and videos showing me how much of a good time they were all having. And a couple of months before this trip, we had all gone to stay at the Legoland hotel and had visited all the attractions in the theme parks.

Mum and I had also started our own little chicken and duck farm and invested in our new babies. We had bought incubators and the chicken broods and had planned everything before we got the eggs to incubate and hatch. I had ducklings and Mum had chickens – she would get so excited about them and when we had our daily FaceTime in the evenings, she would show me her baby chicken moving around in the egg.

"LOOK! That's my little baby in there," she'd say to me whilst squealing with excitement.

When I analysed everything, going over every little thing that had happened during the last year, I remembered the time my mum was randomly sorting her life insurance out. She picked me up in the car after I finished work one evening and was on the phone to them on loud speaker.

"So, if I picked the top package, would it cover mental illness? Because I have suffered with my mental health in the past," she curiously asked the man on the phone. I looked at her and raised my eyebrow, thinking, "What is this all about?"

"I will have to check the policy but yes, I'm pretty sure it does. If a suicide was to occur after a year of you being with us, your pay-out would succeed," replied the man, sounding confident.

"Okay, that's perfect. I'm not saying I'd ever do that, but I'd like to get everything covered as the other day when I got my health check done, I had to tell the lady about my mental health," Mum replied.

Thinking back, I feel so angry at myself – I should have known there and then that maybe, just MAYBE, this was the start of her plan. I mean, was it? Could it have been? It looked as though she was figuring out a plan to make sure we as a family would be alright when she left, but that wasn't the case. Her life insurance never came through. Dad has been left with so much stuff to pay out since she's been gone. She didn't think it through at all. It was so silly of her. In the moment, you don't take any notice of the people around you because you assume that they are okay. You just don't see these things or take notice. Unless it's so visible to the eye, or unless that person is so noticeably depressed, you just don't notice the signs.

It's sad that it has to result in a life being taken for us to care more about one another, it shouldn't be that way. We need to speak more, listen more and just be a hell of a lot more wary about each other.

CHAPTER SEVEN

Spotting The Signs

Grief Lesson # 10:
Don't beat yourself up for not
realising.

I wish I had spotted the signs before it was too late, I wish I had known. Looking back at the months before Mum took her life, there were quite a few signs that she was feeling depressed. I wish I had known what signs to look out for with suicide. Maybe if I knew what to look out for, I could have helped her. It's not easy to know if someone is feeling suicidal – we can't read people's minds, we can't always understand the way that they may be feeling at any moment. It's often hard for some people to express how they are feeling to someone for many reasons. My mum was a very closed book when it came to her feelings – she always put a front on and hid behind a smile. The only person she had confided in, opening up about how she was feeling, trusting him to not tell a soul, was her friend.

The month leading up to Mum's death, she showed quite a few signs that she wasn't coping and, looking back, it was obvious that she was acting out of character. She pushed my dad away and randomly broke up with him, and she tried to avoid phone calls with me sometimes or there was a delay in her responding to my texts. She was shopping a lot more and got herself in a lot of debt (we didn't know this until after she passed away). And Mum was hardly a drinker, she would normally go out once or twice a year for a couple of drinks with her friends, but she started doing this weekly before she passed.

I have done some research and found other signs to look out for, as well as the ones my mum displayed.

Signs to look out for:

- A change in emotion: restless, agitated, aggressive, angry, tearful.

- A change in behaviour: tired or lacking in energy; not wanting to talk to or be with people; not replying to messages or calls.

- A change in language: talking about feeling hopeless, worthless or helpless, and using phrases such as "I don't want to be here anymore", "Everyone will be better off without me", "All of my problems will end soon", or "I want to die".

- A change of routine: sleeping more than usual or not sleeping at all; eating more than usual or not eating at all.

- A change in risk-taking behaviour: such as becoming violent or gambling; using alcohol or drugs to cope with feelings.

Just remember that these signs may not always be noticeable as everyone expresses their emotions differently – they could be really good at hiding how they feel like my mum. If you do spot any of these signs in a friend, family member or loved one, try and encourage them to talk about how they are feeling.

There were also a few other situations that we physically couldn't see with Mum, but later found out she was struggling with. It could be possible that these other struggles, such as financial worries due to her spending, depression, job-related stress and other circumstances, played a factor in her feeling that taking her life was the only way out.

It can also be useful to recognise situations that can trigger suicidal thoughts or make it hard for someone to cope.

Situations to look out for:

- relationship and family problems
- loss, including loss of a friend or a family member through bereavement
- financial worries
- job-related stress
- college or study-related stress
- loneliness and isolation
- depression
- painful and/or disabling physical illness

- heavy use of or dependency on alcohol or other drugs

- thoughts of suicide.

These might not apply to everyone who is struggling, but they can be useful to look out for.

CHAPTER EIGHT

Life Without Mum

Grief Lesson # II:
You may never know the reason.

A suicidal mind can be so many things. It could be the girl who has just treated herself to a brand new outfit. It could be the guy who boasts to all his friends about how happy and amazing his life is. It could be the man who is standing at the bar buying everyone drinks, laughing and smiling away. It could be the teenager who is telling her parents about how great her college life is going and how excited she is for her future. It could be the postman who smiles at you every morning as he hands over your mail. It could be the lady who has just got a promotion at work and whose life seems perfect. It could be the student who is top of their class. Basically, it's not always the person who isolates themselves and hides away from the world with tear-stained eyes, locked in their bedroom with the lights off, trying to battle their evil demons every day.

It could be anyone, at any time, at any place.

When someone you love passes away so suddenly, so unexpectedly, so tragically, it hits you in a different kind of way. It leaves you questioning absolutely everything. You'll find yourself trying to find answers and clues, anything that could help you understand. It makes you feel crazy, like your mind is going into overdrive.

The day Mum died, at about three in the afternoon, I asked my partner to take me for a drive in his car, just to get out of the house for a bit.

"Where do you want to go?" he asked. I remembered where Dad had told me Mum had been found and I asked my partner to drive me there, I wanted to see where her last moments on this earth were, to try and understand why she might have chosen that place.

When we got there, the first thoughts that entered my head were, "This looks so peaceful" as the scene was quiet and there was nobody in sight, no noise but a couple of birds in the trees. It was in the mountains and, on that day, the weather was miserable, rainy and foggy. As I looked out of the window, I soon started to think negative thoughts, feeling upset and distressed; the tears streamed down my face as I observed everything around me.

"She must have been so lonely up here all on her own," I cried out to my partner as flashbacks of what the police officer had told me started to evolve in my mind, my imagination picturing it in my head as I stared out to where her car was last parked, to the place where she was found.

During the early days, I was constantly trying to work out why my mum did what she did. I would sit on my phone, googling why people commit suicide, trying to understand why she felt the need to leave us. I researched for days. I felt like I had to solve this, treating it almost as if it was my own crime investigation. She left no note, no messages to me, my dad or my brothers. She sent my dad a text message when he was a sleep, around 3 or 4am, telling him her life insurance numbers and other important information. She even sent a message to one of her work colleagues the night before she died, thanking them for being such a great person. But not us, her family. And that was pretty hard to comprehend. The only thing she did leave, which to this day I still don't want to listen to due to her slurred words, was a voicemail that she left on her friend's phone, hours before she died.

Why him? Why did he get a voicemail and we got nothing? Were we not enough?

The police gave us the belongings that she had with her that day inside her work car. Dad handed me Mum's white floral Cath Kidston handbag. I held her bag like it was a crown jewel, hugging it as if it was Mum herself. The inside of her bag smelled of coffee – not just any coffee, it was the kind that you smell when you are in the airport. Whenever she came home from work we'd get this aroma of coffee coming from her.

I had convinced myself that Mum had left a note inside her bag for us to read, but after rummaging inside, no note could be found. All that was inside her bag was her water flask, glasses, purse and some other little bits.

Maybe on her phone, I thought. I knew Mum's passcode, as did my dad and eldest brother. I tapped the passcode into her phone. "Eh?" I said out loud, confused at the sight of the code being wrong. I tried putting it in again, maybe I had entered it wrong. But it still wasn't correct.

"Dad, did Mum change her passcode recently?" I asked, my eyebrows raised ever so slightly. I started to think that she may have been hiding something if her phone had a different code now. "No, it's still the same, why?" he replied. "I can't get into it, she's changed it," I stressed. He suggested other possible passwords that she could have changed it to, but after five attempts, her phone was disabled.

Even now, we still can't get into her phone so we may never know what she was possibly hiding.

The morning after my mum passed away, I felt like I had just had a nightmare. Once I had woken up, I was hoping I would find out that none of it was real. I probably had about two hours sleep – me and my partner slept downstairs in the lounge on a smallish blow-up bed. I remember just sitting there on this squishy blow-up bed, feeling cold, numb and nothing but empty, gazing into the distance and thinking to myself, "Is this my life now? Am I always going to be feeling this way?"

For a long time after, Dominic would wait up at night until I had fallen asleep. I used to have nightmares about my mum, especially after I visited her at the funeral home, and sometimes I would wake up either screaming or crying because of a terrifying dream. A year later, I still get the occasional nightmare, but it's not about my mum anymore, sometimes the nightmares are about my partner passing away, or something bad happening to my dad, brothers or even my own children. I think it's a fear of me losing someone else I love.

The skies were dark and gloomy that first morning – strangely, the weather had gotten stormy all of a sudden when Mum died. Dad and I would often say that it was

Mum giving us a sign. Thinking back, we would all often believe that she was around, trying to give us a sign. Maybe she was or maybe we were all just clutching on to anything to keep Mum's spirit alive in our minds.

Every day, getting my dad up and out of bed would be a daunting mission. He was awfully depressed. I had to be the strong one and push my feelings aside and take care of my dad and brothers and make sure the house was still being run. When trying to get my dad up and out of bed he would occasionally say things like, "No, I don't want to get out of bed", "I miss my wife", "Why did she do this?!" It was worrying watching him slowly disappear and turn into a man I had never seen before. I would sit there on the end of his bed, the room dark and lonely, and I'd listen to him cry, talk and shout about how he was feeling. I hadn't witnessed my dad cry since I was super young, probably about four or five; I remember this memory of him sitting on his bed, tearful and upset as he stared at a photograph. "Mum, why is Dad crying?" I had asked my mum and she told me it was the anniversary of his dad's death. It was only after Mum died that he told me more about his dad – he lost him when he was just thirteen years old.

I was able to understand a lot of how he was feeling from the same perspective which was good, because when you've just lost someone you love with all your heart, and you're grieving so woefully deep, you need to feel like you're being listened to whilst you're expressing how broken your hearts is. Even if the other person says nothing back, it feels ten times better to speak about whatever you are feeling inside, to get it off your chest and to feel like you are being heard. I know, because that's how I was feeling too. If it wasn't for my partner being so supportive and understanding, I think I too would have been feeling completely lost like my dad.

Dad, my eldest brother and I had quite a few arguments in the months following Mum's passing. They would be over things so little – for example, a month after Mum died, I had a row with my brother because he had made her desk all messy, and it felt like he didn't care, throwing all of his stuff over it. I shouted at him with all this rage that had taken over me and stormed off upstairs shouting, "I DON'T WANT TO BE HERE ANYMORE!" and I broke down, sitting at the top of the stairs. My dad chased after me minutes later and comforted me. "You're angry and upset because of Mum aren't you?" he asked me. I could hear his voice cracking. I nodded and we hugged, sobbing in each other's arms.

I think losing someone to suicide can make you go through so many different feelings and emotions; it makes you feel angry over everything, even minor things, and it makes you protective over all of their belongings. It makes you jealous when you see people around you being happy. I just wish it didn't have to be this way.

When Dad wouldn't come out of the cave he had turned his bedroom into, I would try to persuade him to come downstairs. I'd make him a cuppa and say, "We'll take one day at a time, day by day things will eventually get better." Dad and I would have a chat most mornings, and he'd tell me how much he appreciated me. "I don't know what I would do if you weren't here Chlo, I'm just so lost, y'know?" he'd sob to me whilst wrapping his arms round my shoulders, hugging me tightly and letting his tears crash onto my skin.

My paternal nan came round every day – in fact, family members from both sides popped in every day for a while to support us, and even neighbours would check in to pay their respects. My mum's cousin, Lynsey, played a huge part in supporting us all after Mum died. And I can't thank her enough for doing so – if it wasn't for her, I don't think my dad would be as okay as he is today. Dad would often mention things like wanting to go and join Mum and not live on earth anymore, but Lynsey would snap him out of it. She called him up several times a day, even messaging me as well to see if I was okay. She'd come over whenever she could, which was mostly every week, and she helped us with closing all of Mum's debts and sorting house bills out, as well as helping us with planning Mum's funeral and many other things.

Lynsey was the first person to see Mum after she had passed. I remember we had all gone to Brighton to go to the phone shop to sort out my brother's phone as Mum was the one who had been paying for it, so my dad had to get a new contract for him in his name.

While we were there, the funeral director called my dad and, because I was the one who wanted to see Mum in the funeral home, he asked to speak to me. I wanted to know when it would be possible to see Mum as it had been two weeks since I had last seen her (this was a week after she had passed away). The funeral director was being very slow in the process of getting Mum ready and said that he wasn't sure when she would be ready for viewing. They hadn't washed her or anything. This made me feel really sad and distressed. All I could imagine in that moment was my mum's lifeless body being all alone. The more the funeral director and I spoke, the words going back and forth, the more frustrated and upset I got. It was almost as if he didn't care. Thank God for Lynsey – she took over with the phone call and sped up the process by going down there herself and making sure Mum was sorted. I can't thank her enough for helping us through absolutely everything. I know other family members were there for us too, but Lynsey – <u>YOU</u> were there with us every step of the way. And you STILL check in on us. You are amazing. You remind me of Mum in many ways, especially with your heart of gold, so thank you.

Five days after Mum passed away, I had to go into work to sort a few things out; it was also a way of getting out the house for a bit and seeing a different face for a change. Mum was found down the road near my job, just round the corner. I will never forget the feeling I got every time we drove up the road to my work after she died, it made me feel sick to my stomach every single time. Every time we reached the road, I'd think about Halloween night, and my mind would spiral as I'd constantly think, "I wonder what was going through Mum's head as she drove up this road", knowing this was the last destination she drove to before she passed away. It was awful, absolutely heartbreaking. I'd stare out of the window with tears trickling down my face, the ends of the sleeves on my top would be soaked by the time I got to work, from wiping away all my tears throughout the car journey.

When I walked into work, judging by everyone's faces, it was as if a ghost had entered the room. Everyone knew, but they had no words. Some smiled, some nodded. I hardly looked anyone in the eye, and tried my best to avoid eye contact as I would just sob at the words "Are you okay?"

But I had made a really good friend whilst working at the nursery, she was so lovely. She greeted me with a hug and cried with me. She could feel my body shaking. I remember telling her where Mum was when the police found her, and that's when she told me that she had seen my mum at the petrol station that evening before she died. It's just so tragic. Nobody knew those were Mum's last moments, well, except Mum herself.

I entered the office and spent a good hour talking to my two managers, it really did help me in many ways. I know I had my partner for support, but speaking to someone who isn't so close to home really makes a big difference. And I don't have many friends, so yeah, it was like a breath of fresh air.

After a month, and after thinking for some time, I came to the decision to leave my job. I couldn't bear the thought of going up that road anymore – imagine walking to work every day and being reminded that this was the road your mum drove up and died just round the corner from. It was just a constant reminder of the worst day of my life.

Exactly a week after Mum died, my partner's family dog died, completely out of the blue. It was bizarre. I was upstairs in my mum's room at the time and I heard my partner come through the front door, sounding out of breath and not himself as he spoke to my dad. I rushed downstairs to see if everything was okay. "Is everything alright?" I asked him, sounding concerned. "Tyson's died," he replied as he wiped his eyes. I could tell he was trying to keep himself together and not make a huge thing out of it because we were all currently grieving.

"Oh my god! I'm so sorry! Poor little pup," I said, as I hugged him. Tyson was the sweetest little rottweiler, the cutest, loving, most handsome little pup ever. The first time I met Tyson was when I went over to my partner's house, I think for the first time (back when he lived with his parents). Tyson scared the crap out of me, waiting for me at the bottom of the stairs, eyes full of anger and barking constantly whilst I descended. I stood behind my partner scared for my life. I was laughing but it was more of a scared laugh. He was probably shouting, "Who the F are you and why are you in my house?!" I gave him ham and from that moment on we became the best of friends.

I also know how it feels to lose a pet – losing an animal is just like losing a family member or friend, the pain feels the same. Of course, we all know pets have short life spans and that eventually their day will come, but we're still not mentally prepared for it. Having them in your life and a part of your family for many years and then suddenly they're not there the next day hurts just the same as any other loss. When you are used to waking up in the morning and your normal routine of going downstairs and being welcomed by their cute little face smiling at you with their slobbery tongue sticking out, wagging their tail as you talk to them in your baby voice; their cheekiness as they try and sneak around you, scavenging for scraps as you eat. It all leaves a huge gaping hole in your life when they're gone. We lost our family dog Quest when I was pregnant with my daughter. Quest had grown a huge tumour on her face, just behind her ear (it was literally the size of another head) and unfortunately it was inoperable, it had gone too far which meant she had to be put down.

The evening Quest passed away we all sat down on the floor kissing and cuddling her, we sobbed for a good while before the moment she got the injection from the vet that sent her to pet heaven. It felt like the grim reaper was waiting outside for us to say our goodbyes, it broke my heart.

The first few months following Mum's death I dreaded the thought of getting married, having another child, going on holidays and everything else that should involve Mum or genuinely being happy. Because Mum was not only my mum, but she was like my best friend and we literally did everything together. She wouldn't miss any moments. She was a planner and was very organised, and now she's not here I feel like everything is so out of place and messy. She was so hardworking and devoted to her job, and she was such a boss woman (quite literally). I loved her motivation to always work towards something higher. She achieved so much over the years. It's just hard to understand that my mum had everything, but she still felt like she was nothing.

After I announced the news on social media about Mum, I noticed that some people would appear then disappear like a magic trick. I had gotten people messaging me with support. They would reassure me with messages like "always here if you want to talk". But when I would actually reach out to those people after Mum's funeral had been and gone, when I really felt like I needed someone to talk to other than my family, hardly any of them replied. Leaving me unread. Not even a message later in the week to check in on me to see how I was coping.

The only time people did want to talk and I'd receive any kind of messages of support was when I'd post a photo of Mum, announcing her birthday or how crap it was that she wasn't here on Mother's Day. Basically, anytime I'd speak about Mum on social media, that's when people would reappear. It's almost like everyone forgets the next day as they get on with their lives. When this happened, I'd feel bitter and jealous. Maybe because while my family and I were sitting here, grieving this awful loss of our mum, the people around us weren't hurting like we were. Maybe I just wanted everyone to feel the pain we were feeling, just so they could understand. I know how busy life can get, we all get tangled up in our everyday routine, too exhausted to contact anyone by the end of the day. But if you have told people that they can rely on you and come to you for a chat whenever they feel like it, and you have seen their message pop up on your screen, please stick to your word and reply.

I remember back in February, it had been three months since the loss of Mum and I had gone back to my home after staying with Dad for the past four months. It was evening time, around 5pm, and I was cosied up on the sofa, just finishing some food I'd had for dinner. I went onto my phone and saw an article about a TV presenter called Caroline Flack who had committed suicide. I didn't really know much about this TV presenter, I just knew of her and that she had presented a few shows. But as soon as I read the article, and the more I read back through it, my heart just sank. I could feel myself welling up because everything with Mum was still very raw. It really hit home for me. I thought about how heartbroken her family and friends must feel – losing someone so suddenly is awful. I couldn't stop bawling my eyes out after I read it – it had reignited the fire of grief in my heart.

I had this one friend who had been a really good friend since we were kids in school – we'd speak all the time, supporting each other when she had her children and I had my first daughter. When I told everyone the news of Mum passing away, she messaged me with support and offered to meet up so I could get out of the house. But obviously the last thing I wanted to do whilst I was grieving was to meet with anyone for a coffee. I felt that seeking a distraction from my grief was some kind of act of betrayal. The pain inside me would make me feel angry, sad and depressed. I didn't want to see the people outside smiling and enjoying themselves.

When Mum's funeral came along, this friend said she'd be there. Her mother joined us, but my friend was nowhere to be seen. I didn't even get a single text from her explaining why she wasn't coming or even to say she was thinking of me on the day. I felt disappointed. Maybe she didn't have the words to message me and was afraid of upsetting me. But take this tip from me – always always message, don't avoid it. Even if you are afraid that your words may upset that person, it is much better than not speaking to us at all. We still haven't spoken to this day. And to be honest, it is what it is. I only have time for people who have time for me.

CHAPTER NINE

Where's Nanny?

Grief Lesson # 12:
Let others take care of you.

One of the worst parts of grief is both that the world stops, and that life still goes on. The next day, bills still have to be paid, dinner has to be made, the children still have to be taken care of. During the worst part of my life, I was lucky to learn exactly who I could depend on: my partner's family.

I am so fortunate to have Dominic's family available most of the time and thankfully they looked after our daughter for a while so I could grieve properly. No child should witness their parent's grief, I wanted her to be as far away from this situation as possible.

A few days after my mum had passed, Dominic and I visited his parents' house so we could spend some time with our daughter. I had to buck up the courage to explain to her about why Mummy was upset, which also meant telling her where Nanny had gone. I remember holding the tears back so hard, I could feel my ears burning red hot and the feeling of having a lump in my throat, as if a golf ball was about to choke me.

As soon as I entered the house and saw his sisters and parents open their arms to me, I welled up. My daughter was playing with her toys at the time and I gave her a cuddle straight away. "Mummy why are you crying?" she asked. "I'm sad because your amazing nanny was really poorly, the angels have taken her up into the sky and I miss her," I replied. She was nearly three and understood well but I don't think that she fully understood the implications of what I told her, which I'm so glad about – she didn't get upset, couldn't feel the pain that we were feeling. I'm so pleased that she wasn't able to feel that pain – I wouldn't wish this on my worst enemy. She gave me a cuddle and wrapped her arms around me and that made me feel instantly better – children don't realise how much a hug from them makes everything just that little bit better when you feel like your world is crashing down around you.

Visiting Dominic's parents and sisters was daunting at first because I was afraid of crying in front of them, I didn't want people feeling sorry for me, but it was such a relief in the end, and I left their house feeling like a huge rock had been released from my chest. My partner's mother felt like she could sympathise with me, as she too had experienced the loss of her mother, so she knew how it felt to lose a parent. She sat and cried with me, telling me that she knew how painful it was right now, but reassuring me that it does eventually get better. In that moment I could only think and feel the worst – how could I move on without my mum? How can I ever be happy again?

The first time my daughter actually asked me where Mum had gone was roughly a month after she passed away. The dreaded fear of having to re-explain why Mum wasn't going to be coming back was like someone sticking a needle into my skin, repeatedly pricking me over and over again. I was still staying at my dad's house so obviously my daughter must have thought to herself that Nanny would be back soon – why else would we be at her house still?

"Mummy, when is Nanny coming back?" my daughter sighed, her innocent blue eyes gazing directly up at me, tugging at my shirt. I explained to her that Nanny was poorly so the angels had to take her up into the sky to look after her. But you know what children's curious minds are like with their 101 questions – it was obvious for her to assume that Nanny would be back soon. Children in their total innocence are completely oblivious to the sad things that can go on around them sometimes.

"But Mummy, when the angels have taken care of her and made Nanny better, they can bring her down again, right?" she mumbled whilst fiddling with her toys. Her response had thrown me a little, and I tried to think of something fast to prevent her mind from speculating.

"Darling, Nanny isn't able to come back home because her new home is with the angels up in the clouds. The angels have asked Nanny to help them with a big job. But whenever it's night time and we see a twinkly star in the sky, that's Nanny looking down on us," I replied, trying my absolute hardest not to shed a tear.

My daughter speaks about Mum most days; she has a desk that is placed next to a window in our living room, and whenever she does her drawings, which is most days, she looks out of the window, watching the birds in the trees and the clouds drift in the sky. One time she said, "Nanny is always looking at me being a good girl isn't she Mummy?"

And just when I thought my shattered heart couldn't sink any lower, here it was, like a rusty old padlock was attached to it, weighing it down to the bottom of the gloomy, cheerless sea. Hearing her say that with her sweet, honeyed voice hit me like a freight train. My mum would always tell my daughter how much of a good little girl she was. "Are you going to be a good little girl for Nanny?" she would say. I can hear her high-pitched voice in my head as I write this, the way she'd speak to my daughter in her baby voice. My daughter would be so excited when we would see my mum, her voice would instantly screech "Nannyyyy" when Mum picked us up in her red work car. I'm so glad my daughter was able to spend the first couple of years of her life with Mum, and it's amazing how my daughter remembers the memories made with her too.

When my daughter was a baby, just a couple of weeks old, my mum would look after her whilst my partner and I would catch up on sleep for an hour upstairs in Mum's bedroom. Because diving into being a first-time parent is hard work and exhausting. Oh, the sleepless nights! Mum would be thrilled to watch my daughter, especially overnight. She would record numerous videos of my daughter, reassuring me that I wouldn't miss any special moments. In one video, she captured my daughter's windy smiles and my mum's voice in the background can be heard saying, "Say Mummy, I'm making Grandad work. He's in the kitchen making me a top-up because just one bottle of your milk wasn't enough." She then chuckled with her cheeky laugh and proceeded to say, "I'm still hungry and I'm going to give them hell tonight, or just Grandad anyway. Smile for your mummy! Say I love you!"

It's just a great pity that my daughter and son won't be able to grow up with Mum around, having that person other than me to go to for advice when they reach their teens. Because Mum gave out amazing advice all the time. Although my children have my dad and their other grandparents around, it still hurts for me.

There is no better feeling making your heart warm, than seeing your own mother with your children. I would sit and gaze at Mum whilst she played with my daughter, showering her with doting love. Sometimes being cheeky and passing her the odd sly piece of cake or a little treat, thinking I wouldn't notice.

(Yes Mum, I totally saw that, but no I won't tell you off because grandparents are supposed to spoil their grandchildren.)

My daughter is four now and she loves speaking about her nanny and I'm so glad that she was able to gain some memories with my mum and is able to talk about them so clearly as if they had only happened yesterday. My son, who was born in November 2020, will never get to meet his nanny and form that special relationship that my daughter had with Mum, which crushes me every time I think about it. He'll never get to hear Mum's hilarious laugh, see her cheeky smile, experience her warm, loving cuddles or be able to create those fun memories with her.

Now Mum isn't around and able to do all these things, it just means I will have to make it my absolute mission to keep her spirit alive by sharing photos and videos of her so they can hear her cheeky laugh and see her smiley eyes. I envision the time when my children are old enough for me to gather them round and tell them stories of their hilarious, mischievous grandma who is hugely missed every day.

CHAPTER TEN

The Funeral

Grief Lesson # 13:
Don't let fear control you.

Before my mum's funeral I visited her twice at the funeral home. The first time I saw her I went with my dad, Lynsey, and Lynsey's mother. I had to sit down with my dad before I went in, I had so many thoughts racing through my head. I remember sitting down outside the room my mum was in and thinking to myself, "Surely Mum can't be in there, this has to be an awful mistake." My dad said to me, "You don't have to go in there if you don't want to." I was anxious and I kept getting the shivers. It took me about five minutes to build up the courage and pull myself together and go in. My dad didn't come in with me as he couldn't face seeing Mum, so I went in with Lynsey at first. Before Lynsey opened the door I asked if Mum looked okay, because I know that our bodies do deteriorate quite fast. "The bridge of her nose is slightly bruised but she looks fine. Are you ready?" she replied. I nodded and Lynsey proceeded to open the door.

That moment will never ever leave my memory, as I walked into the small, candle-lit room, where Mum's coffin was placed to the right of me. I first noticed her coffin lid leant against the wall, it had her name written on it with her date of birth. It was slowly hitting me. I then noticed the top of Mum's black hair straightaway. I was shocked, and my eyes were watering up as I looked directly at Lynsey. I felt the urge to cry but I just couldn't, nothing would come out. Had I run out of tears? Or was I just too shocked at the fact that I was looking at my mum in a coffin right now? I was shaking, feeling emotionless and I couldn't quite believe she was actually lying there. As I looked at her, lying ever so peacefully in her coffin, it felt like I wasn't actually looking at my mum, it was like I was staring at someone else, like a relative of my mum's. Mum was dressed in the long black dress that I had picked out for her; the fact that the dress was actually brand new with the tags still attached says a lot about Mum – she always overbought new clothes because she loved shopping. I mean, who doesn't, right?

At first, I couldn't touch her, I was too scared, afraid even. Lynsey helped me place mine, my dad's and my brothers' separate letters under Mum's hands. We all wrote our own letters to Mum, none of us had discussed with each other what we put inside our letters as it was our way of talking to Mum on our own. For me, writing a letter had helped me get what I wanted to say to her out of my mind and off my chest. Dad kissed his letter to Mum before handing it over to me. I could smell his cologne on it – he had sprayed Mum's favourite one all over the letter, just for her. We brought one of Mum's Mickey Mouse teddies which had a photo on it of all of us in America, along with a Mickey Mouse pillow and a Stitch ornament as she did love her Disney films and she loved Stitch. Lynsey placed all of these in Mum's coffin for us.

As I sat next to Mum, staring and inspecting her from top to bottom, I thought to myself "You're so silly," thinking that she'd hear my thoughts. Lynsey and my great aunt and I all sat there reminiscing about Mum. I had never seen someone in their coffin before, but it felt like I was just visiting Mum in hospital; it was a very odd experience.

Before we left, my dad was asked if he wanted to see Mum, and he decided that he did. He came into the room, touched Mum's face and gave me a cuddle and cried. He held me so tight, I could feel him shaking as he squeezed me ever so tightly.

As I went to say goodbye, I touched Mum's icy cold hands, stroked her hair and said, "Sweet dreams Mum". And then I kissed her forehead.

As I walked out of the room, I instantly felt like a little bit of weight was lifted off my chest. I got the closure I needed, and I'm glad I had that last moment with her. I felt as if I had to go visit my mum because if I hadn't seen her, in my mind I would forever have thought that she had taken off somewhere. I wouldn't have had any real closure had I not gone to visit her.

I really thought I'd cry when I visited her, but I suppose the shock of it all delayed my feelings. Even the second time I saw her to say my last goodbyes I still couldn't quite believe it. But as soon as I had a second on my own and a moment to think and take it all in, it all caught up with me and I ran upstairs and locked myself away to be on my own and cry in my mum's room.

When you're crying with such intense grief it's a totally different feeling of crying. It's deep and your chest is tight like someone's stopping you from inhaling air. Your mind feels hazy like your brain's gone to mush, and you feel a numerous amount of emotions but all you want to do is scream and shout and hope for someone to give you answers.

Mum's funeral was the second hardest day of our lives. On our way up to the crematorium I looked out of the limousine window, trying to distract myself from shedding a tear whilst my partner held my hand, rubbing my thumbs with his as he tried to silently comfort me. I saw people living their life in the streets, smiling away while we had entered our own personal hell.

I could hear my dad sniffling behind me, gasping for air. My youngest brother who was seven at the time was saying to my dad, "It's okay Daddy, I'm here", "It's okay to cry." Dad crying in the backseat was enough to set me off. A little tear would escape from my eyes, but I was able to just about hold myself together. We arrived at the church and the hearse with Mum inside was parked directly in front of us, her favourite cream-coloured roses lying upon her coffin. We all broke down. I tried to catch my breath, feeling like my heart was about to explode from my chest. My partner was even wiping his eyes too. There was no dry eye in sight; we all sobbed like the day we found out all over again, realising that in just half an hour our mum would officially be no longer here.

The funeral proved just how loved my mum was – there were so many people who had turned up to show their respects. Most of her work colleagues, friends, and our family all joined us to say our last goodbyes. The church was so full of people who loved Mum and wished to say goodbye that a fair few had to stay standing, that is just how many people turned up.

After we all sat down, the ceremony began and the song "A Thousand Years" by Christina Perri started playing. My mum's work friend was the minister and gladly offered to lead the funeral. After she had read the introduction and a part of the Bible, she began to read out the eulogy that me, my dad and my brother had put together in tribute to Mum.

A tribute for Mum

Dad: "For those who don't know me, I am Peter. We started dating 24 wonderful years ago, making her my wife on the 2nd of August 2008. We met at work whilst I was a chef, and she was a care assistant. I knew early on that I wanted to spend the rest of my life with her, we had good and bad times but that's normal in a long-term relationship. I never stopped loving her and will never stop loving her. She gave me three wonderful children who we love dearly. We also got a lovely granddaughter from Chloe who Sandra loved with all her heart. Sandra was a massive Disney fan and looked forward to family holidays to Florida to spend, spend, spend. Her favourite character was Stitch who was a little mischievous alien. I could see the similarities in Sandra as she too was mischievous. You could never lose Sandra. She had a very loud laugh which when she was young, she sounded like a seal. A loveable one at that. Sandra had an obsession for stationery, with the amount she had you could open up a shop.

Sandra was very strong minded so if she wanted something, she would try her utmost to get it, eventually getting what she wanted. Once she asked me for a new computer. I said no so she calmly got her handbag and softly bashed me with it chanting puter, puter, puter, continuously until I gave in. Needless to say, I always gave in to the woman I loved, she got the computer.

She was very professional in her career, excelling throughout the years, gaining numerous qualifications and rising to the position of area manager for children's homes. She loved what she did, and I would always support and praise her in what she did. Sandra was the most beautiful caring person you could hope to meet. She would always put other people's needs before her own and I loved her for this. I think we all did. She was strong willed, loving, loyal, passionate, most of all she touched the hearts of everyone she knew. There will never be anyone like her which made her so special. Your legacy will live on in your children and grandchildren. I am a broken man now that my better half has gone. The only comfort is that I can see her in the faces of my children. Her family was the most important thing to her; without them she was nothing.

Rest in peace my beautiful wife until we meet again, I will love you for eternity. Your husband, Peter."

Chloe: "My favourite memory with Mum was when I gave birth to my daughter. Mum was so supportive. She spoiled my daughter rotten and treated her like she was her own. Mum wasn't only my mother, but she was also my best friend. We would always FaceTime each other every day and chat about absolutely anything for at least a couple of hours, planning trips to Ikea and counting down the days until the weekend and especially what we both wanted to buy, as most of you know Mum loved shopping! I will miss your smile, your laugh and the love that you gave us all. I wish I could give you one last hug, as whenever you'd hug me, you'd squeeze me really tight and tell me how proud you were of me and that you loved me. Your granddaughter knows that the angels are looking after you and she always gets your photo and gives you a kiss. I love you to infinity and beyond.

Sleep tight angel. I will see you again one day."

Chris: "I will always cherish the moments with Mum. For the times we always tried to make each other jump around the house, for the times when we had fun on rides in America and one time Mum was so scared on a ride, she felt like she was going to fall out of it, and it made me and Chloe laugh a lot. Mum and I would always make fun out of each other and I would often sit on the end of Mum's bed and watch films with her and occasionally rub her feet for pocket money! Thank you for everything you've done for me Mum. I love you."

After the eulogy had been read out, the song "With or Without You" by U2 started playing. I wept and grabbed my dad's hand who was sat beside me; my daughter who was sat next to me on my partner's lap also cried. She's very advanced for her age and I think she kind of knew what was going on, that we were saying goodbye to her nanny.

It was time to put our roses on Mum's coffin, time to say our last ever goodbye. My dad and brothers went first and went up to Mum's coffin, and each placed a rose on top of the wooden casket. I remember watching my dad place his hand upon the coffin, his head bowed down, wiping his tears away, almost too afraid to let go and say goodbye. I remember feeling the heartache for my dad; watching him cry broke my heart every second – it felt like my heart was made out of cotton and someone was cutting each strand bit by bit.

After my dad and brothers sat back down, it was then mine and my daughter's turn to say goodbye. As I stood up, it felt like everything had gone into slow motion. I looked at everyone around me; my anxiety was high, my heart thumping hard in my chest. "Say love you Nanny," I said to my daughter, as my partner picked her up so she could place her rose upon the coffin. I kissed my hand and placed it on Mum, talking to her in my head, only assuming she could hear my thoughts.

As the curtains closed on Mum, the last song started to play: "When you Wish upon a Star" by Disney. I remember hearing the intense cries all around me. When almost everyone had left the church, I followed and was soon surrounded by people who had lined up to offer their condolences. I looked around for my dad but then found out he had stayed inside. He wasn't ready to leave Mum yet so he went behind the curtain to say goodbye privately one last time.

Mum had left Dad a widower, just about to enter his fifties, all alone. Going back home to a house that feels quiet and empty without her, although my brothers live there too; he will forever feel lost without her. My eldest brother was about to turn eighteen, a month later. Celebrating his first-ever birthday without her here. And also leaving my youngest brother, who at seven was too young to understand, without that mother figure around anymore.

We spoke to nearly everyone who attended the funeral, thanking them for coming and paying their respects. It's all a bit of a blur but I do remember being so overwhelmed by it all. I don't remember many faces or conversations, I just remember a lot of hugging and crying.

We had Mum's wake shortly after the funeral, and at the wake I had laid out a Disney memory book on a table for everyone to add their messages to Mum inside. Some people also brought photos to stick inside too. We asked everybody to take one of Mum's roses with them before going home so the flowers didn't go to waste, and we also had a donation box for people to donate money which all went to the suicide prevention charity.

As the night went on I drank enough to numb the pain, not crazy drunk but just tipsy enough to be able to get past the hurt that was inside my chest. Dad did the same, and if I'm honest I think it was good for him to have that heartache of his numbed as well. It was nice to see him relaxed again, back to his own self. Although he had cried many tears throughout the evening, he deserved to be able to smile, to reminisce and talk about Mum whilst smiling, without gasping for air as his heart would shatter.

Towards the end of the evening, I was speaking to a good friend of mine who is my children's godmother. We sat at the table, talking for quite some time. I told her everything that had happened, all of the details. She held my hand whilst giving me good advice, reassuring me that things will eventually get better. Telling me that she will always be there for a hug, cry, anything.

I also remember my uncle coming over to me before he left that evening, telling me how beautiful my daughter was, especially her big blue eyes. Explaining how nice it was to finally get together again, even if it was under such tragic circumstances. He gave me a hug before he left. Over the past years I had longed for this moment. My mum never knew, but I so desperately wanted to speak to certain people again on her side of the family, but didn't because I didn't know how it would make her feel.

I think the best thing to have come out of Mum passing away was that I was able to reconnect with my uncles and other family members. I had seen family that I either hadn't seen in a long time or had never even met before. It was a very special day that I'll never forget.

I will always grieve my mum, and I'll always be sad and upset that she's not here.

The pain will never go away but eventually, I'll learn to live with it without shedding a tear or feeling like my heart is about to shatter every time I think or speak about her.

CHAPTER ELEVEN

Receiving the 'Box'

Grief Lesson # 14:
Research and prepare yourself
beforehand.

A week or two after Mum's funeral, we got the call from the funeral directors to go and collect Mum's ashes. I had been dreading this day ever since the funeral. Dad, Lynsey and I all went together. Before we went to collect them, I wasn't sure what to expect. I don't remember the funeral directors giving us a leaflet or explaining to us what to expect when collecting a loved one's ashes. What would the remains be stored in? Are the ashes heavy or light? I think it would have been useful for the funeral directors to have explained what to expect prior to collecting, that way we could have all emotionally prepared ourselves before our arrival. Some people may think "they're just ashes" but the thing is, unless you've lost someone and had them cremated, you need to remember that once upon a time these ashes were a human being, living life just like me and you. And this specific person had a beautiful soul.

We sat at the round mahogany table in the dim-lit quiet funeral home waiting for the funeral director to sort everything out. I looked over at Dad who was sitting beside me with his bloodshot eyes due to the daily crying, hand on his head, staring into the distance, looking like he was a million miles away.

When the lady gave us Mum's ashes, she was in a cardboard box with her name printed on it. She also gave us a lock of her hair along with her fingerprints on a piece of card. My first thought when I had Mum placed right in front of me inside this box was, "How can someone you love be here one minute with us, alive, and then the next her whole self is granulated and placed inside a small box? Just how?" It's awful.

As I carried Mum's heavy box of ashes back to the car, I felt like the outside world was dull and meaningless. Although that day the sun was shining, most of my days felt like cloudy, miserable days with a pinch of storms thrown in.

When we got back to Dad's, he told me where to put Mum for the time being. He didn't want her where she was visible because it was too painful, so the best place was inside the Disney cabinet that was full of all her Disney ornaments and collectibles. This was the same cabinet where our late family dog Quest's ashes were also placed. Before putting her in the cabinet, I sat there for a few minutes, staring at this box that Mum was in. I placed my hand upon her and I don't know if this was my brain tricking me but the box felt a tad warm, like she was still here. It comforted me at the time anyway.

I had seen a movie once where a woman had collected her husband's ashes and she had opened the window to let his spirit free before placing him inside his urn. So I thought this was a thing. Maybe it is, maybe not, but it sounded like a natural thing to do. So I opened Mum's box, not expecting her to be in a paper bag inside the box. Then I went to open the bag and Mum's ashes started to spill out, so I freaked. I ran downstairs and said to Lynsey, "So, I tried to let Mum's spirit free out of the window but she's spilling out of the bag." Lynsey smiled at me and said, "Ah that's alright, I'll come and help you." And so we let her spirit free together. Fly high angel.

A year later and Mum is still in the cabinet. Our plan is to get her into her urn by the end of this year, followed by eventually making her a memorial garden with her ashes placed there too. And soon, when the time is right, I will be able to bring some of her to my home. But for now, it's too heartbreaking. Dad has never seen Mum's ashes and I don't blame him. I found it really bloody hard seeing my own mother inside this box. Dad has come a very, very long way from where he was when Mum first died. But he still can't even have photos of Mum hanging downstairs or in his bedroom – they're all up on the top floor where my brothers' bedroom is and Mum's office.

Nothing has changed much back at my parents' house. Mum's clothes are still hanging up in her wardrobe and every time I go in her office where her wardrobes are, I sniff her clothes as well as her favourite perfume, it just makes me feel close to her, like she's still here. Her office is exactly how it was when she first left it. We have moved things that she left downstairs and in her bedroom into her office because they were a constant reminder that she wasn't here anymore; we just wanted to ease the pain in our hearts that little bit.

Of course, there will always be a constant reminder of Mum at the house, nothing can change that, she ran that house like a queen. I remember when I was 16 and living with my parents and I'd be up in my room being a typical teenager, locking myself away. Throughout the day I'd hear Mum shout up the stairs saying, "Chlo!" and then I'd shout back "Yeah?" and she wouldn't answer (being a typical mother) or she'd ask for hangers or for help with preparing dinner, anything chore related really. I miss hearing her call my name or shout demands up the stairs.

CHAPTER TWELVE

Uncommunicated

Grief Lesson # 15:
Be wary of those you trust
around you.

A few weeks had passed since Mum's funeral and one evening I went onto my laptop and finally got into her Facebook. I immediately clicked onto her messages, hoping that I could find some sort of answers as to why she felt like she wasn't good enough for this world. I just wanted to try and put myself in her shoes.

I found a chat between her and a friend, the same friend who had called me on the morning Mum died. The only person she had spoken to in regard to her feelings was this friend, so I clicked on their conversation and proceeded to read.

Starting from October the 29th at 7am, three days before Mum passed away.

For the confidentiality of this person, I have renamed my mum's friend Donald.

Donald: You ok?

Mum: No

Donald: Oh dear, that's not good. What's up?

Mum: Battling old demons. Sick of being in my own head. Tired of the same shit over and over.

Donald: Yeah, I get you on that one.. It's like, haven't I fought you enough over the years? please just leave me the fuck alone already.

Mum: Yep, just want it to end already. Over this shit.

Donald: The sad truth is, it will never totally go away, but you find new and better ways of dealing with it.. and once you start to find yourself a bit more, then your mindset will change, and you'll find things a lot easier.

Mum: It's not about finding myself Donald, it's just the bullshit family I have and the fact that everyone I trust and love fucking hurts me, don't see the point.

Donald: Well, that's not entirely true is it, yes most of your family are dickheads but you've got your 3 children and grandchild. They all give you strength in times like these... And I'm still here for you... you know that, you're going through something very difficult at the moment with massive life changes, there's going to be times when it's a struggle and when you get past the worst of it then you'll see just how strong you are, there is always a point, just sometimes you have to look hard to find it, but once the storm clears, you'll see things so much clearer, I promise.

Mum: (shrug emoji)

Donald: Trust me, things will get easier and you'll see.

Mum: Yep.

Donald: Your answers aren't filling me with confidence that you are really listening or want to talk.

Mum: You have no idea Donald, no idea at all.

Donald: Well, tell me then, it's gotta be better than keeping it in.

Mum: Don't know what to say Donald, I just.

Donald: ..?

Mum: Just want this all to stop.

Donald: It will take time to feel that you're making progress in your new life changes. Whatever you do, don't give up. I'm free Thursday, I'll pop down for a chat and a catch up if you like?

Mum: No

Donald: Ok, well what would you like to do? you can't just message me like that and not expect me to worry or want to help you. You are my friend and I care about you, if you don't wanna talk to me, will you talk to my friend if I ask her... She's a really good listener?

Mum: No

Donald: So you just wanna shut off and do exactly what you moan at me for doing. you need to talk to someone it will help just to let it out.

Mum: (shrugging and crying emoji)

Donald: Always here if you wanna talk but I can't make you, like I said my friend is a girl and been through some really really rough times. Worse than me she has said in the past. If you ever want to talk to her she would be happy to listen. it doesn't have to be if you don't want it to be.

Mum: (crying emoji) It's easier to push people away.

Donald: Don't I fucking know it. But it's not always the right or best choice. sometimes just a little chat can make all the difference.

Mum: I'm just so tired Donald.

Donald: I get that, you're fighting yourself all the time and with work and the kids, it's a lot to do on your own.

Mum: Sorry x

Donald: Don't ever be sorry. You've got nothing to be sorry about.

That was the end of the conversation that day.

As I was reading these messages, I felt sad. Sad because I couldn't believe I didn't notice how depressed she was feeling, she was so bloody good at hiding her emotions and making everyone believe that she was happy.

The next day, the 30th, my mum had asked "Donald" to come round to her house in the evening.

Mum: Are you busy tonight?

Donald: No not now, what's up?

Mum: Don't Worry.

Donald: No, I've made myself free. What's up?

Mum: No, you don't have to as I don't want to feel a burden or anything and I already feel like that (Sad face emoji)

Donald: Don't be silly. you're not a burden, the same as when I feel like that I'm told I'm not one either. now would you like me to come down tonight for a chat or did you have something else in mind?

Mum: I don't know, I just feel really shit and keep crying and I'm struggling right now not to cry. Just feeling like I'm losing my shit right now.

Donald: Ok I'll come down yours and you can talk, cry and share your struggles. It might really help.

Mum: Hey, I don't want you to come down if it's going to affect you in any way, as that will make me feel worse if I've affected you too. (sad face emoji)

Donald: No. That's not how friendships work. I told you I was here for you and I meant it, I'm here to help if I can.

Mum: Yes, but I don't want to make you feel crappy, fuck. I don't even want to feel anymore.

Donald: I'll be ok, it's you I'm worried about.

Mum: (shrug emoji)

Donald: What time do you want me to come down then?

Mum: Any time after 7.

Donald: Ok, see you about half 7-ish then.

Mum: K.

When I had read these messages, I started to get a little annoyed at Donald. Why didn't he notify at least my dad about how my mum was feeling? Surely if your friend had told you that they were struggling and they didn't want to feel anymore, your first thoughts would be, "I should really contact someone about this". Because maybe someone else other than him could have helped Mum.

The next time they spoke was on October the 31st at 9:35am, the day before Mum passed away.

Mum: Hey I just wanted to say I'm really sorry, you don't need my shit and I don't want it either. Just wanted you to know I value our friendship and don't take it for granted. Sorry x.

Donald: There is no reason to apologise, and I'm here for you whether it's in good or bad times, that's what friends do. And I don't see what you're going through as shit. it's a struggle right now but it will get easier... and I'll be there to help as much as I can until you don't need me anymore.

Mum: Thanks, I'm going out later anyway.

Donald: Oh, where you going? and I hope it's to do something positive, not something else.

Mum: Pete's coming round after work to see the kids and spend a few hours with them so I'm going out for a drive.

Donald: Ok. Just, is there a friend you can go see? so you're not alone or pop round Chloe's or something?

Mum: Can't Donald. Anyway, I'm fine. It's all going to be fine.

Donald: Yeah, but your idea of fine and mine may be very different... you need to be around people, it doesn't matter in what sense but you need to be not alone.

Mum: I'm fine.

Donald: Bollox... don't be trying to fob me off, if you were fine then you would want to go see a friend or Chloe.

Mum: I'm fine. Sorry x.

Donald: I don't want you to be sorry. I want you to let others help you.

Mum: I'm going to be fine.

Donald: Yes, I hope you are.

Mum: I feel so torn right now.

Donald: Yeah I know you do, just keep focusing on your kids and granddaughter. It's what will save you, do what I said and tell Peter that you can't go on the holiday as you just can't do it right now. let him decide what he wants to do and just get that weight off your shoulders... It's only a small thing but you need to start somewhere.

Mum: (Shrugging emoji)

My mum and dad had booked a trip to Las Vegas for my dad's 50th birthday, but at the beginning of October they had hit a rocky patch in their relationship, this is why "Donald" had suggested to Mum about telling my dad that she didn't want to go on the trip.

Donald: Trust me, it's what anchored me when I needed it, and if you do go driving around tonight be extra careful as all the kids will be out trick or treating.

Mum: I'm not going to be driving where there is kids around, but I am going out as soon as Peter comes round. I can't be there and don't want to be there. I just don't know what I want to fucking do, I have this horrible feeling

---

100

which I can't describe in the pit of my stomach. just feel I'm being pulled in two different directions right now.

Donald: Yeah and that's perfectly fine to feel that way. After everything you've been through and how it's all coming back to the surface right now, like I've told you it's at your weakest that these things attack your soul but you'll be ok. Just hang in there ok? don't give up.

Mum: (Facepalm and crying emoji) Feels like I'm at the top of a bridge right now and not sure which way I'm going to fall.

This for me really hit hard. Man, if I was her friend speaking to her that night and she had told me this, I would have called either myself or my dad immediately, or at least tried to persuade her to come and meet me.

Donald: Always lean back towards the people that matter the most.

Mum: If I was a true friend I wouldn't be involving you in my shit, as I said earlier I don't even want to deal with it anymore, so I shouldn't put it on you too.

Donald: Are you joking... that's exactly what real friends are for, the good and the bad so don't ever think you can't bring your problems to me.

Mum: Donald, I just feel like damaged goods right now. I've just got home so I'm just gonna get ready and go out before Pete gets here.

This was the moment my mum had told me via text that she had reached her home and was going to call me back when she was sorted.

Donald: Yeah and I do get how you feel, in respect to being damaged goods that is. Ok get ready, go out. But play happy music in your car and drive to somewhere that reminds you of a happy memory.

My mum was found at the same destination where we had taken our family dog Quest on the last walk of her life before she had passed away. Did "Donald" really just help my mum choose a place that she would spend the last seconds of her life at?

Mum: Yeah right.

Donald: Do it. Happy songs bring on happy feelings, and it will help your subconscious.

Mum: No.

Donald: It will. And ok just put the radio on then, that way you'll get a mix of songs.

Mum: Whatever.

Donald: Look, you can be as moody as you like and as closed off as you like but it won't change the way you feel or the fact that I'm still here for you, just so you know that ok.

Mum: I'm not being moody, I'm fucking scared of myself right now. I just need out.

Donald: Yeah you will, you're just struggling with it all at the moment, give it a little time and you'll find a way you can talk about it and release some of that stress, anxiety and all of them other emotions that are eating you up right now.

That last message from "Donald" was sent at 6pm. Mum didn't reply until 8pm, starting a different conversation. I would assume at this time she was driving around trying to find somewhere to go. I can't imagine the thoughts that were racing through her mind.

Mum: You totally underestimated me.

Donald: In what sense?

Mum: It doesn't matter.

Donald: Yeah it does.

Mum: It really doesn't.

Donald: Ok. What are you up to?

Mum: I'm sorry Donald, I really am.

Donald: Don't be sorry, just hang on in there and never give up, that's all I ask.

Mum: You can't ask that.

Donald: Yes I can, and I will as I don't want you to do anything silly and you can't take back.

Surely this shows that "Donald" had a suspicion that Mum COULD possibly do something unreversible? Why oh why didn't he tell anyone about this?

Mum: (Shrugging emoji)

Donald: No it's not. this is just a bad chapter.

I then came across a message that enraged me. I started to get a sweaty forehead, my blood was boiling. My ears felt warm to the touch. I was frowning with anger so hard that if it was possible to throw daggers out of your eyeballs, I would have broken my laptop screen.

Mum: Should of let you take it yesterday.

Donald: Yeah you should have, them pills won't help you, and you don't need them.

Mum: But now.

Donald: No, don't take them. you need to go home and look at your kids. If you're at home then go just sit with them for a while to get some perspective.

As I was reading these messages, the more I scrolled down the page, scanning the conversation, I could feel my head warming up even more, a wave of rage coming over me. "WHY!" I shouted, slamming my hand down onto the table.

Just why didn't her friend tell us?! I was livid, confused, and betrayed in a way because he was a friend not just of my mum, but of my dad too.

Mum: I'm not at home, I left them with Peter.

Donald: Yeah, but what time is he leaving?

Mum: I asked him to stay the night as I said I was going out and didn't know when I would be back. He then had a go at me

Donald: Why did he do that?

Mum: (Shrugging emoji)

Donald: What did he say?

Mum: Why does it matter, it doesn't matter.

Donald: It does matter you div.

Mum: Do you really want me to call you back?

Donald: Yeah, if you're not home. I need to know you're safe.

Mum: Well I'm not home.

Donald: So ring me then, so you're not on your own

"Donald" then sent Mum four different memes, presumably trying to cheer her up. Was this the best he could do? Did he really think sending memes would make someone who felt this low, this broken, snap out of wanting to take pills? I was literally face palming at this point.

Mum: I'm sorry, bye x

Donald: Oi that was not a very nice way 2 say bye. Please go home.

Mum: No Donald, I'm not being horrible I just can't do this.

Donald: Fine don't go home, but just don't do anything silly. you can do this, you've proved it in the past.

It baffles me why he didn't think to either tell any of us or to call the police immediately. She could still be here today if he had just told somebody.

Mum: As I said earlier, you underestimate me right now. I want to say goodbye properly. You are a great friend and couldn't wish for more. I'm just so fucked I can't xx

"Donald" didn't reply to Mum's last message which was at 2:37am on November the 1st. She tried to call him an hour later but he didn't pick up.

Mum was pronounced dead at around 8am, after the paramedics tried to resuscitate her.

"Donald" had been a close friend of my mum and dad since way before their wedding in 2008. Their friendship had gotten stronger since "Donald" had broken up with his wife and my mum had been there to support him and cheer him up as he started to feel depressed himself. She had invited him round to her house with my dad, taken him out to watch films at the cinema, and then in the months leading up to her death, she had started making drinking into a hobby, going out more often with him. This was out of sorts for her because she wasn't much of a drinker. "The taste of it makes me sick," she'd say when we'd have conversations about alcohol. I'd tease her with one of Dad's Jack Daniel's bottles, opening the lid and trying to make her sniff it. She would pull this face that almost made her look like she was about to gag; it used to make me chuckle so much.

Knowing that my mum had gone to this friend and left voicemails before she died made me ask myself, "Were we not good enough?" For a while, I thought that. Because we never got a note, a text, a voicemail. We got nothing, and my questions will never be answered because only Mum knows why she didn't leave us a letter. Maybe she has and we are yet to find it but it's very unlikely. I think she was way too sad and more determined to get rid of the pain. I don't think she was thinking clearly and had her mind so focused on doing this one thing that she had been planning to do.

In my opinion, I think when two people are depressed and hang out with each other, it becomes less of a support system and more of a toxic and unhealthy friendship. If both people are full of negativity then they are unable to help each other because they are both upset and full of toxic thoughts, and when you are surrounded by negativity, you take on that sadness. Both people need positivity in order to feel better.

In the end, I think no person, nothing, could have made my mum feel better. She probably realised that not even her friend's company was able to make her feel better.

You're probably wondering if I ever confronted my mum's friend about why he didn't help her that night.

I wanted to call him up so bad and to shout and scream at him from the top of my lungs, begging for an explanation as to why he didn't help her. He was the last ever person who spoke to her before she died, he had the opportunity to save her, but he didn't.

The thing is, I knew he was depressed too and I would have never been able to forgive myself if he had harmed himself in any way because I had made him feel worse about the situation. If I were him, I would feel awful knowing that I could have done more.

It was already too late to change the way things had panned out; Mum had already done what she had done.

It was unfixable.

Instead of starting an argument with him about the situation, I just blocked him out of my life to prevent any further contact. I think deep down he knows he could have done more to help her. We all think that we could have done more. Hell, I thought about how I could have done more, called more, texted more or even visited more. Every. Single. Day. For months.

The last time I saw Mum was a week prior to her death.

All we can think now is that our mum isn't in pain anymore, but no, she's not in a better place because the best place for her is with her family. It's just such a damn shame that she couldn't open up to any of us, HER

FAMILY. She was so good at acting like she was happy, you couldn't tell any difference in her voice.

That's the thing with mental health, you really don't know what goes through someone's mind.

On the outside they could look so happy, like they have everything they need, but on the inside they could be in so much pain, fighting the demons away.

CHAPTER THIRTEEN

A Letter To My Mum

Dear Mum,

It's been just over a year since you left us. Some days it feels like it was only yesterday that it all happened and other days it feels like it's been forever since I last hugged you.

There is SO much I wish I could ask you and speak to you about. I miss gossiping with you and having our daily FaceTime calls. I don't have my best friend here anymore to go out on shopping hauls with and to tell me if a specific outfit looks good on me, or anyone to go to the salon with and get our nails done together. I don't have my mum here to love and comfort me, giving me the best advice, have a rant with, go late night shopping with. No one to drive to random places in the evening because it was relaxing to just go out on a drive. I miss watching you be an amazing nanny, and it's disheartening knowing that you'll never meet your grandson and he'll never get to meet you. I can't visit the same places that you and I visited in the past, because it causes too much pain. The holidays will never be the same because YOU were the one who brought everything to life. Without you there is no joy, you were the joy in all our lives.

I always speak to you in my head or when I go up into your office, hoping I'll hear your voice speak back to me. I always assumed throughout the past year that your ghost self would appear, or that you'd give me some sort of sign that you were near.

I hope you don't mind me taking your grey knitted cardigan

that you wore all the time, it's very snug! Although, as I write this I can hear you in the back of my head saying, "Oi you cheeky moo!"

My therapist asked me a question the other day. She said, "If you could speak to your mum right now, what would you say to her?" Firstly, I would probably spend the majority of the time crying, because I've not been able to speak to you for a whole year. Secondly, I'd ask you why you didn't feel like you could talk to us. Why couldn't you open up to us about your emotions? Why did you only speak to your friend and not us? Why didn't you leave us a note? I will never hear your answers and over time I will accept that you most probably felt too sad to say goodbye to us. It breaks my heart to know that you felt that the only way to stop the pain was by taking your own life.

Mum, if I had the chance to speak to you, I would tell you just how loved you really were. I would remind you of how much joy you brought to everyone's lives with your contagious laugh and infectious smile.

I'm so sorry that I didn't notice how sad you really were feeling. You were so caring towards everyone else as well as putting on a front and trying to prove to everyone that you were strong, but in reality you were breaking down, day by day you were slowly chipping away.

I wish I could go back in time to when you were here. I wish I had called you up repeatedly after you didn't answer my call the first time, just to say all of these things to you. If only I had known then about how you were feeling.

We all need you.

Dad's hoarding of trash is getting out of control, honestly his excuse every time is, "Well Mum isn't here to tell me off now so I can do as I like." Apart from that, he is still running the house just the way you liked it. He really misses you Mum, he will never stop loving you. He told me the other day that his heart will always belong to you.

I will always be left with so many unanswered questions. I never got one last hug or kiss, I didn't even get to say goodnight before you left. You said you'd call me back but you never did.

I don't know if anything I could have said to you would have made a difference because I couldn't feel your pain, I didn't know what demons you were facing on a daily basis. But I can only hope that it might have changed your desire to leave us.

I love you more than you will ever know. I wish you knew that this world was not better off without you.

You will always live in me, the boys and my children.

Love Chlo xxxx

CHAPTER FOURTEEN

Hello?

Grief Lesson # 16:
Face your fears.

A couple of weeks after we had picked Mum's ashes up, my brother Chris was upstairs in his room. I was downstairs in my youngest brother's room settling my daughter into bed as we were still staying with my dad at the time. All of a sudden, I heard my brother yelp in a high-pitched voice.

"Chloe! Chloe! Get up here now!"

I steamed up the stairs; my brother shot out of his bedroom as I reached the last step.

"Did you hear that?" he asked, looking scared stiff.

His body was flinching as he edged towards the bathroom.

"Hear what? I heard you call me but I was downstairs," I replied.

"I was in my bedroom and I swear to god I heard Mum screaming through the bathroom air vent!"

I chuckled at him as I try not to believe in ghostly things otherwise I would become an anxious little scaredy-cat.

"Shut up, you must have heard a fox howl or something."

"No Chloe, it was her scream," he said in a serious tone.

A few days later, another mysterious incident happened, yet again in the evening. My brother witnessed his games and his other belongings being swiped from his TV unit and falling onto the floor. Coincidence or not, but maybe it was Mum hinting to him to tidy his room for once.

I didn't really think anything of this "scream" or his stuff falling onto the floor that my brother kept going on about, but obviously I wasn't there to witness it so I couldn't say if it was real or not.

But just before Christmas I was sitting downstairs in the lounge with my brother, reminiscing about the good old days of us with Mum. We were speaking about whether ghosts were actually real since Chris really believed he had heard Mum "screaming" through the bathroom air vent. Mum would totally scare the hell out of us for a laugh – the number of times I'd come out of the bathroom and Mum would be hiding behind the door, nearly giving me a heart attack by screaming at me to make me jump, or hiding behind the wall as I'd come down the stairs, screaming with pure horror. My brother and Mum would have scare wars most days. These moments were countless.

That evening, while my brother had gone upstairs to fetch a game we were about to play on the PlayStation, Mum's desk chair started randomly rocking back and forth on its own – it wouldn't stop creaking. My whole body froze completely stiff – I couldn't even bat an eyelid. I'm one of those people who freeze if I hear a slight noise whilst trying to sleep, hardly able to blink, with my heart racing a million miles an hour.

"Chris, hurry up with that game!" I shouted whilst keeping my eye on the chair.

He ran downstairs sounding like a herd of elephants were following him.

"What?" he replied in his deep, blunt voice.

"Mum's chair was rocking on its own, and the arm rests were clicking," I told him, almost laughing because we are both little scaredy-cats.

"Nope, no thank you, I'm out," he said, as he walked out of the room, too scared to be in the lounge with Mum's alleged ghost.

Dad walked in minutes later and asked us both what we were scared about, he could hear us from the kitchen. So I told him about Mum's chair rocking back and forth and then Chris mentioned about Mum's scream in the air vent that had happened previously. Dad laughed. "What, so you think that's Mum trying to scare us do you?" he chuckled, as he spun her desk chair and then slumped himself onto it, in complete disbelief that ghosts were real.

It wouldn't have been the first time she'd scared us that's for sure. Eh Mum?

My brother also told me about the time when he was in his room playing his PlayStation whilst speaking with his friend over the phone. He was sitting on his bed, chatting away and all of a sudden he felt something tug the bottom of his jacket; he shrieked with fear and turned around to see what was tugging him from behind, but nothing was there.

The more these mysterious incidents kept happening at my dad's house, the more I'd start to believe them. One evening when I was at home cooking dinner in the kitchen, I felt something warm on my shoulder, as if someone had touched me with their hot hands. I turned round assuming my partner was behind me but I was the only one in the kitchen. I stood there for a good couple of minutes staring out into the hallway, baffled as to what had touched my shoulder whilst my chicken was sizzling in the pan on the stove. It really does make you wonder.

Are ghosts/spirits real? Or is this our minds playing tricks on us? Maybe we believe that all these little things are Mum because we want it to be Mum, to somehow feel as if she's still here with us even though she's not physically here.

Somehow, it's comforting even if it's a little freaky.

CHAPTER FIFTEEN
BETTER TOGETHER

Grief Lesson # 17:
It's okay to be angry.

Since Mum's been gone, my relationship with my dad has gotten a lot stronger. I had always been a daddy's girl when I was little, giving him more affection, hugs and love. But as soon as I had hit my teens, the conversations with Dad became dull and blunt and I'd find myself always turning to my mum for advice or for an opinion on something.

My dad, being the typical man he is, didn't really show much interest in things like "does this top look good on me?" or my shopping haul, or as Mum used to call it my "hinch haul" as she was totally obsessed with the fabulous Mrs Hinch on Instagram. Dad would just shrug his shoulders and go "that's nice" in the most casual, uninterested voice ever whilst raising his eyebrows to make it look like he was interested. Anyone else's dad do this? He does give amazing, thorough advice when it comes to cooking though, so that's super handy.

Dad and I are both good at expressing and speaking about our emotions, unlike my mum and brother who are very much the opposite, and like to keep it all inside.

I visit my dad every week now; he'll normally pick me up, and as soon as I step foot in the car it's like he views me as one of his guy friends, chattering on like there's no tomorrow. It's as if a fizzy cola bottle has been shaken to the max and the cap launches off. He talks to me about Mum all the time, and I think the reason why he speaks so much about her to me is because he can't speak to my youngest brother, who's now eight, as he's too young to understand, or to my other younger brother, who's nineteen, because he's not good with talking about Mum or emotions. So I think he bottles his emotions up until he sees me.

When he takes me back home again, he often gets weepy during the journey and says, "I wish she was still here, I miss your mum so much," holding the steering wheel with one hand, whilst wiping his watery eyes under his fogged-up glasses.

"I know you do, I miss her too," I reply, keeping myself together because if I cry, all hell will break loose and we'll both be ugly crying in the car which is no good for either of us.

Dad has also helped me so much since Mum passed – in his words, "It's what Mum would do if she was here". And that couldn't be any truer. Dad took me to my pregnancy scans when my partner was unavailable, he bought the baby his crib and whatever I needed, always giving me a lift to wherever I needed to go. He even listens to my little life dramas and reacts the way Mum would have done.

He really has stepped up, being both Dad and trying to do Mum's role. You are amazeballs, Dad!

My brother and I have gotten a lot better at not fighting every time we see each other as well. Our relationship has reached the stage where we can actually get along and laugh about everything. Whenever I go round to Dad's, he leaves his little mancave and sits with me and talks all day. He talks to me the way he used to talk with Mum, throwing banter at me left, right and centre. When he feels like he needs to talk about his thoughts and how he feels, he confides in me, which I'm so glad he can do now. A year or two prior to Mum's death, he wouldn't be able to talk to any of us, not even Mum, so that's a big achievement.

Him and Dad both have something in common which is replying to text messages within two or three working days. It's okay though, when I don't get a text back, I just call the house phone until someone picks up – Mum used to do this too, because men are the WORST when it comes to answering calls and texts, am I right?

My dad and my brother have on and off rows which result in me sitting down between them both so they can talk it out and get to the bottom of why they keep rowing. I feel like a therapist as I tell my dad to speak in a calm voice and my brother to apologise!

Overall though, all our relationships have grown stronger and we've gained a stronger connection through this loss; we talk a lot more than we used to and we can also relate with each other to how we feel since losing Mum. But it isn't the same as talking to Mum herself. I miss going on shopping hauls with her, speaking for hours on the phone, sending each other funny memes over text, gossiping about the latest news and the smell of her Paco Rabanne Olympea perfume lingering around the house.

My brother probably misses being able to laugh with Mum, playing around and making each other jump out of their skin. Sitting in her bed with her watching TV programs whilst Dad was at work, enjoying each other's company.

My dad probably misses going to bed with her by his side every night, her laughs, smiles, the way she'd pick the gross spots on his face even though he'd scream like a girl every time she'd gouge them out of his nose with her spot tool. Our holidays. The list goes on. But most importantly, he won't be able to grow old gracefully with the love of his life.

The truth is we all have different things that we'll miss about Mum. When she died, I tried to attach to people who were like her in some ways, trying to find a mother figure who was like her. For example, my mum's cousin Lynsey; I slowly attached to her and would ask my dad when she'd next be visiting us, getting all excited like a little kid when she was coming round. I snapped myself out of it quick enough though.

The reality is that nobody can ever BE like Mum or THINK like Mum. Because Mum is Mum and she's irreplaceable.

CHAPTER SIXTEEN

The New Normal

Grief Lesson # 18:
Give yourself time to adjust to
the new normal of your life.

When our lives were still awfully raw and everything hurt, going outside into the real world without Mum was painful. Every place we'd visit, supermarkets, certain shops, places we'd drive past on the roads, everything seemed to be such a Mum trigger.

You know when you can't have something and then coincidentally, that's all you ever see when you go out for a while?

When Dad and I visited Brighton mall for the first time without Mum, we saw so many happy families walking by. I got so jealous of the other girls with their mums – all around me were mothers and daughters out on their shopping trips, laughing and giggling, the daughters arm in arm with their mothers. It felt like it was being rubbed in my face, the fact that I don't have a mum anymore and that what I see is what I'm missing out on, and I would never be able to do this with my mum ever again. It was like a punch in the gut.

I'd instantly feel such intense anger coming over me, like fire in my eyes, followed by silent cries.

All the memories of me and Mum having mother–daughter days out would come flooding back.

I absolutely miss having a girls' day out. We'd often get pampered at the salon together, getting our nails done, facials, lashes – the lot! A few years ago, Mum would only go to the salon if it was for a special occasion like our birthdays, or if we were about to go on holiday. But then after a while we started going every couple of months to wind down, relax and use the opportunity to have a good old gossip without the children distracting us.

I used to hate going if it was for pedicures – yes, I'm one of those people who hate feet! I can't stand the thought of people touching my feet, it makes my stomach churn! Buuut, Mum used to always persuade me to get them done. "Come on Chlo, you'll have lovely toe-nails when they're finished!" I remember how we'd dip our feet into the foot spa massager and look at each other, giggling at the foot massager tickling our feet, like little schoolgirls. And then I'd throw the odd banter at her about her funny toes and she'd say with a soppy, but giggly voice, "Oi, don't take the mickey out of my toes!" I crave these girly mother–daughter days every single day.

A daughter will always need her mother, no matter how old she is.

A month after Mum died, Dad and I went out Christmas shopping to the mall, because who else was going to buy the children's presents now Mum wasn't here, filling up her trolley to the max?

We were a couple of mopey sloths walking down the streets in what felt like slow motion. I remember feeling so emotional at the time that if the store worker asked me how my day was going as I walked into the store I'd almost blubber. I think we only went to the mall that one time and did the rest of the Christmas shopping online because it was too painful, walking the streets where memories were made with Mum.

Mum would go absolutely crazy at Christmas time – even on my first ever Christmas when I was only four months old, I had a ridiculous amount of presents piled around the Christmas tree. As the years went by and Mum was buying for more children, the pile grew higher. When we were old enough though, Mum would get us to work for our money, making sure we learned that money doesn't just get given to us for free.

Not long after Mum died, I was walking down the street after dropping my daughter off at nursery. As I stopped at the traffic lights, waiting for that little green man to appear, a small red car stopped behind the line. I remember my eyes widening and my gut dropping as I caught a glimpse of the woman inside this small red car, with long black hair and a fringe, wearing sunglasses. She looked exactly like Mum. But of course, it wasn't Mum. This woman wasn't listening to "NOW That's What I Call Music" bangers in the car for starters. You could hear Mum's music from miles away – no, honestly, it was so loud it could deafen you.

This happens quite often when I'm out – I see someone who looks like Mum, with her black hair and bouncy fringe, and then I realise she isn't here anymore. All I ever see now that Mum's gone are red cars, it's like my eyes are constantly scanning the streets looking for Mum's red work car. Because that's the vehicle she would pick me up in 90% of the time. Even a year later, my poor old brain is still scanning for her red car to screech round the corner, beeping to tell me she's outside.

Every day for a while after Mum died, I would read back over the text conversations between me and mum. It would bring comfort to me as I'd lie there reading them during the night when I couldn't sleep, smiling and reliving the messages, as a tear drop would slide down my face. These messages are the closest thing I have left to speaking and having conversations. I'm so scared that my memories of our face-to-face chats will slip away. I'm scared to lose bits of my mum.

When you have everyone you love in your life and nothing could be any better, you take things for granted, you don't realise that all of these special moments you have with your loved ones could be snatched from you in an instant. I just wish I had a time machine to turn back time and redo everything, making sure I cherished every little moment I had with Mum.

My youngest brother, who was seven at the time, started having nightmares shortly after Mum died. He would wake up screaming with terror and crying; he'd tell Dad that he'd had a nightmare about Dad dying. He still gets nightmares now, he goes through phases of them. When you lose a parent that young, the after effects are hard for their little minds to handle.

I learned early on that I couldn't flick through photos of Mum without becoming sad and crying, it all felt so surreal. A day after Mum died, one of her best friends sent me a photo of Mum taken a week before she passed – she looked so happy. But sometimes I found comfort flicking through them at times when I did become upset. On the other hand, watching videos of her alive and well, seeing her smile and hearing her laugh, was a whole new level of torture. I couldn't watch videos of her without shedding a tear, having that lump in the throat feeling that just won't go away.

A year later and I can happily look through photos of Mum, reminiscing about old times with my daughter or partner, but it still pains me to watch her in motion, alive and well.

My dad still isn't able to look at Mum's photos to this day, it shatters his heart all over again and puts him in an awful mood, making him take a few steps back after this long journey he has tried so hard to get by.

I also find listening to songs makes me break down in tears – that doesn't stop me from listening to them though. One afternoon, I was in the kitchen cooking dinner. I had asked Alexa to put on a Disney soundtrack for my daughter (or was it for me? You'll never know because, yes, I love Disney songs too!), and along came the Phil Collins' song "You'll be in my heart" from the film "Tarzan". Now, when I say I was hysterically crying on the floor, slobbering and snotting into my red checkered tea-towel, believe me, it wasn't a pretty sight. It wouldn't surprise me if my neighbours had heard me to be honest.

It wasn't the last song to set me off – a year on and I'm still crying at songs. I can't even have the radio on in my partner's car without blubbering. I try to either wear sunglasses or avoid all eye contact with him and just stare out of the window until the car journey has finished.

But believe me, a good old cry is just what you need sometimes. It does help, I promise.

CHAPTER SEVENTEEN

It's Just A Dream

One thing that has been a very long-lasting effect for me since Mum died is having nightmares/dreams. I thought that this would go away after her funeral had been and gone but even a year on, I still get two or three nightmares a month. These are always about either Mum or someone else I love and, unfortunately, they always end with death.

The first nightmare I had about Mum happened a few nights after she passed away. I vividly remember it. I was running up the stairs to get away from Mum as she was chasing after me. I was running away from her and she was saying, "Come on Chloe, stop running. I just want to talk to you" in a creepy, cheery tune. I remember in the dream I felt anxious, knowing that it wasn't Mum, it felt like someone was controlling her. As I locked myself in the bathroom, she tried to bang the door in, shouting, "Just come with me Chloe, you'll feel better if you do." I don't remember much else happening except before waking up, Mum grabbed me and said, "You're coming with me." She took me with her into what I assume was supposed to be heaven. Except this heaven wasn't a place that seemed calm with angels everywhere. It was quite the opposite. The skies were dark and foggy, and this place seemed miserable and sad. There was nobody to be seen, not even my mum, it was just me in this lonely place. I remember waking up and screaming. My partner woke up seconds after I screamed and cuddled me, telling me everything was okay and that "it's just a dream" as he stroked my head whilst I tried to go back to sleep.

Another nightmare that has stuck with me is about my partner. For some reason in this dream we are living in some huge caravan. He has died in the bathtub. I remember intensely feeling all this pain in my dream, the same pain that I had felt when Mum died, as I saw my deceased partner lying in the bathtub. Later on in this awful nightmare he was alive again, walking around as if nothing had happened. But he didn't look right, his stomach was turning black and his insides were rotting, coming out of his bellybutton. It was an awful nightmare that I couldn't wake up from. As soon as I eventually woke up, I shot up, rubbed my face and made sure my partner was still breathing as he lay sound asleep next to me. I had another dream about him days later where he was dying from a heart problem but he never told me because he didn't want me to get upset or hurt my feelings. Again, the pain feels so real when you're dreaming. Isn't it crazy how our brain makes our dreams so realistic?

I don't know why these nightmares keep happening, I don't know if they'll ever go away either but unfortunately these are the after effects of losing a loved one to suicide loss so unexpectedly. Your brain wonders every day. My mum is the first person I think of when I wake up and the last person I think of before I go to sleep, so maybe my brain is so set on making dreams based around the loss of my mum. I just wish I had positive dreams instead of having these intense awful nightmares that never leave my memory.

CHAPTER EIGHTEEN

Time To Talk

Grief is a really powerful emotion and after losing a loved one your sadness can feel soul crushing, like your world is over.

There is never a "right" time to seek professional help – some people choose not to speak to a therapist because they may feel that it won't work or, in my case, because they feel that they don't need help or that they have a fear of embarrassment. At first, I told myself that I wouldn't want to speak to someone because it felt silly talking to a complete stranger about my personal life whilst they took notes on their little notepad – what are they even writing anyway? Are they drawing doodles? Who knows.

I started having my therapy sessions a few months after the first anniversary of Mum's death. I thought it was about time to speak to a professional, seeing as my mental health was still up and down and I'd often feel like I had two personalities.

One side of me felt able to cope. I would be feeling like I was happy and able to actually smile and laugh without the guilt seeping in telling me that I don't deserve to be happy. I was able to go about my day, felt motivated to do things again, was able to enjoy days out with my family again.

But then the next minute, something would trigger my sadness and it would barge in and push my happy side away. I'd feel like everything was going wrong with my routine for example (sleeping too much). My anxiety would go sky high and I'd normally decide to stay in at all costs because I didn't want to see people outside, my heart would start to crumble again with all the emotions rushing through, and I'd feel like I had just found out that Mum was dead again. Since her death, I have felt alone with everything. I know I have people around me, but deep down I feel like a part of me is missing – because before, I had spoken to her every single day. This new routine, this new life, is just so very different from what I'm used and I'm still adjusting to it.

I have worked out that the triggers that make me feel overwhelmed and angry are mess in the house and something of Mum's or something Mum had given me being destroyed – for example, I got really upset when a coffee mug that my mum bought me years ago got broken. I would get defensive if my partner drank out of a cup of my mum's too.

My therapy sessions took place over the phone due to COVID. In my first session, we started by discussing what my main goals were for when we finished my six weeks of therapy. We then started digging deep into my past, speaking about my childhood traumas and then slowly moved onto the topic of my mum. There was an odd few moments of silence when I had responded to the therapist's question about Mum – maybe she was writing notes or maybe she was trying to think of something to say. But it made me feel that I had said something wrong or that she was waiting for me to say something else. I don't know why, but at the beginning it felt like I was being interviewed. But after the first ten minutes, I got into the flow of speaking about everything and the words just kind of poured out of my mouth.

When we started speaking about Mum and her death and how my life has changed dramatically without her, my eyes slowly filled up with tears, blurring my vision as I held my little three-month-old son in my arms. If I had been in the room with the therapist, I probably would have cried my heart out, but I was at home with my hands full, as usual.

Whilst talking about my past, my therapist said that people who have had a bad upbringing have got a choice and that is to take the bad stuff that has happened to them and turn it into something better. My mum in that case took her bad childhood and turned her life into something better. She raised us and helped take care of the children she worked with in the children's homes. She treated people how she'd want to be treated.

I mentioned to my therapist that every day is like a glass that fills up to the top, and if it overflows then that's when I explode, getting angry about everything. I feel like I have to vent to someone every day about how I feel just to empty that glass. She said that anger is part of the grieving process. I thought I had finished with the grieving cycle, but she said that you never get over grieving and you can experience any part of grief any time after loss, it will go at times but then come back to bite you.

My therapist told me about a few grounding techniques to help me get through my anxiety when I feel overwhelmed.

The first technique is a beathing exercise where you breathe in for two seconds and then breathe out for four.

The second technique is called a 5-4-3-2-1 exercise.

I recommend doing this technique after completing the breathing technique, as it distracts your brain from the problem and calms you down.

Acknowledge FIVE things that you see around you. For example when I did this in my bedroom I saw the bed, washing basket, wardrobe, baby's crib and my TV.

Acknowledge FOUR things that you can touch. For example, I could feel my hair, the hairband on my wrist, the pillow and the floor with my feet.

Acknowledge THREE things that you can hear. This can be any sort of sound, for example if you can hear your stomach rumble then that counts. I could hear the birds outside tweeting, my four-year-old playing with her toys and the TV.

Acknowledge TWO things that you can taste or smell, so you can imagine the taste of your favourite food or go grab something to eat. For me, I could smell the detergent coming from my clean washing that was drying on the airer.

The last step is to think of ONE good thing, for example I thought of my two children smiling.

These are the two methods I was advised to try and they have really helped me when I start to feel overwhelmed.

After speaking to my therapist, it feels like a huge weight has been lifted off my chest at the end of each session. I was able to speak without a care in the world, without worrying what the therapist may have thought about me. Maybe it was easier to speak about it all because it was over a telephone call and I couldn't see her face, or maybe it was the fact that she was a total stranger and she didn't know anything about me.

Therapy is right for some people and for others it's not. For me, it's helped me to be able to cope with the overwhelmingness of it all.

From my personal experience, never judge something until you try it.

CHAPTER NINETEEN
Celebrating Without Loved Ones

When you have lost a loved one, celebrating special occasions and events without them is painful, especially when it's the first time. I wish you could just press pause on the grieving process during these special holidays.

Christmas 2019, only a month after we lost our mum, was really tough. It was the first special occasion we had to go through without her. If it wasn't for my brothers and daughter being there, I don't think there would have been any point in celebrating Christmas at all, but for the children's sake we did it.

We didn't put up the decorations until the week before Christmas Day, and when we did, it was so strange and it just didn't feel right, because we were decorating our family Christmas tree without Mum who absolutely loved the festive period. We are so used to doing these things together and now there's one person missing, and it feels unusual.

Our usual Christmas decorating day when Mum was here would involve getting the decorations out at the end of November or even sometimes as early as the middle of October because Mum couldn't wait any longer. Our day would consist of watching Christmas films while we all took part in decorating the tree and then we'd make mince pies afterwards.

But the first Christmas without her we could just about put the tree up. Decorating the tree and celebrating Christmas in general felt so odd, empty and pointless. I know Mum would have wanted us to do it, but it was just too soon after she had left and it was really upsetting.

We didn't completely decorate the house like Mum normally would, but at least we did the tree for Mum and the kids. We still put a Christmas film on while we decorated the tree and we put all of Mum's favourite decorations on the tree which were her Disney baubles and ornaments.

I got gifted a beautiful tree decoration of Mum to put on the tree from a little business, so I placed her right at the top where the angel would have been.

The week leading up to Christmas Eve, we received a huge amount of help from Mum's work. Her amazing colleagues had gifted presents to the children and to myself and dad and also helped us with getting food for our Christmas dinner. I will never forget the help they gave us when Mum passed. They were so generous, they helped with Mum's funeral and so much more.

On Christmas Eve, I took on Mum's role and made sure the stockings for the kids were filled up; I even filled my dad's stocking to cheer him up a little. I typed up and printed out the kids' letters from Santa and put them in the letterbox to show the kids that Santa had posted his letters and they were so happy.

That's all that mattered really, that the kids were happy. We put out a carrot and a mince pie with some milk for Santa too, and Dad read the children a story before bed, the same Christmas story he read to all of us when we were kids.

That night, after putting the kids to bed, I went downstairs to help Dad finish off wrapping the presents and displaying them around the Christmas tree. I made me and Dad a Bailey's hot chocolate and we both sat down in the lounge and spoke about how rubbish it was having to do Christmas without Mum, reminiscing about old times. When we were kids, Mum would completely spoil us rotten, making sure that we got everything that we asked for – we were those kids who would have presents stacked so high in front of the tree. One present from Santa and the rest from Mum and Dad. As a child, I remember the excitement of waking up at stupid hours in the morning on Christmas Day, I'd sneak into my brother Chris's bedroom to wake him up so we could go into our parents' room and open up our stockings. It brought my mum so much joy when she'd watch us open our gifts, repeatedly thanking them for getting us the toy we had begged for. The only times Mum would really go out and spoil us was on special occasions, even Easter she'd go all out.

The house was quiet which is what makes home feel so empty because Mum made the house feel full with her presence – her loud giggle and her constant calling our names up the stairs as she'd ask us for a favour, her loud screams when she'd watch a thriller or even speaking to the actors on the TV when she was so engrossed in the programme. I'd sit there sometimes and be like, "You know they can't hear you right?"

On Christmas Day it didn't feel like Christmas, it felt like a casual normal day. I didn't want to get out of bed, nor did I even want to open my presents. If it hadn't been for my partner making me get out of bed by shaking me and excitedly saying, "It's Christmas Day" like an excited little child, I don't think I would have gone downstairs at all.

Dad didn't have any motivation to do anything, because why would you want to do anything when the love of your life isn't here anymore? I can still remember and hear Mum's excited little laugh as she'd shout up the stairs saying, "It's Christmassss!"

That morning, after I woke Dad up, we all sat on my parents' bed like we did every Christmas morning and let the children rummage through their stockings, opening up their little presents.

It took time and some persuading to get Dad to open his stocking and get out of bed, but when he did get up, he got out his video camera to film, as he would every Christmas.

We all went downstairs and let the kids rip open the wrapped-up door – it was our own Christmas tradition to have the door that led to the Christmas presents wrapped up. Dad would normally wrap up the door leading to the lounge but he wasn't up for doing it so I did it this time. Once we got into the lounge, the children unwrapped their presents first and I was just happy to sit there and watch the kids and my partner open up their gifts. I told my dad to put the camera on the side and open up his presents. He didn't want to at first and I know how he felt because I felt the same – like I was watching everything around me happening but quietly. I kept looking around the room as I didn't know what to do with myself, I was lost. Mum was the boss of everything and always had a plan for what she was going to do. I think both Dad and I felt off-track.

My partner had got a present for me, my brothers and Dad to open. I was really nervous to open it. I already knew deep down that it was something in relation to Mum. I don't know why but I just felt sad to open it – little things to do with my mum made me realise that she wasn't coming back. When I opened it, there was a big frame and loads of other prints – my partner had named a star after Mum and we had a certificate and other bits that came with it. My dad burst into tears and it was sad to see although he was happy with what my partner had gifted us.

The month prior to Mum passing away, we had been discussing what presents we wanted for Christmas. She had also asked what my daughter would like, so I had sent her a list and she also told me a couple of things she wanted for Christmas as well. A couple of weeks before Christmas, we found some presents stashed in the bottom of her wardrobe from her to the kids. We wrapped them up and even labelled them saying they were from Mum. Dad still labels presents from Mum and writes our cards from her, but he adds a halo at the top of her name which is so sweet.

My first Mother's Day without Mum was a difficult day for me, because as well as having to spend it without my mum and not being able to speak to her, I also wasn't able to spend it with my dad and brothers either due to isolating because of the coronavirus outbreak.

The countless times that day I looked at my phone and looked at her number; knowing I couldn't call her really hurt. Mum didn't even have a voice recorded message on her phone so I couldn't even listen to her voice when calling her.

The day was full of crying, cuddling my daughter and FaceTiming my dad. I'm most thankful and appreciative of my partner for being there to help and support me through it.

On a normal Mother's Day, I would have woken up to a FaceTime call from Mum. 'Happy Mother's Day!" she'd say. We would then discuss what time I would be coming round as she would be eager and excited to give her gifts to me.

Last Mother's Day in 2019, I remember giving Mum her Mother's Day gifts the night before the actual day. I had handmade her a hamper full of gifts of everything she loved – I had completely spoilt her and I am so glad that I went over the top, because unfortunately that was our last Mother's Day together. I would give and do anything to go back to our last Mother's Day just so I could cherish every moment of that day and make it extra special. Extra hugs, kisses and laughs. Now that I don't have my mum around for Mother's Day anymore, I often question myself – what's the point? It's a miserable day for me; not having your mum around on Mother's Day, or any day in general, is just sad. You feel content when your mum's around, like everything is going to be alright.

But I think every time we celebrate these special events we are going to have to make it that bit extra special. Because that's how Mum was, she was always doing things over the top, she loved going all out for everything.

Mum's Birthday, May the 2nd 2020. This day was a hard day because Mum wasn't here to even celebrate her own birthday. On the morning of Mum's birthday, my nan, who is my dad's mum, dropped round some lovely flowers. The funny memory about flowers that always comes to mind and makes me chuckle is that whenever we would buy Mum flowers, they would never survive – Mum would somehow always end up killing the poor things in a matter of days.

In the afternoon, Dad and I baked Mum's favourite cake, which was carrot cake, and for the evening we ordered Mum's favourite takeaway which was a Chinese. After dinner we put candles on top of Mum's birthday cake, placed some photos and candles around the cake, and then we all stood around the table and sang happy birthday to her.

Happy 42nd Birthday Mum, we love you so so much xxx

There will be so much that Mum will miss now, and that's what's sad about having to celebrate these occasions without her. Having to do life without Mum is going to always be so damn hard.

A year on now and we are still learning. Learning how to be a family without Mum being here, making this a new normality. There will always be a missing jigsaw piece to our puzzle. And like I said in my first chapter, one day I can feel completely fine and at peace with Mum's death, then the next day the pain will jump back to me, that heart-wrenching feeling, knowing she isn't coming back.

The first year hurt so much; at times life felt pointless. But it eventually got that little bit easier, just a bit. If you could see me now you wouldn't have thought I had lost my mum a year ago. Yeah, of course hearing my mum's name and talking about her still makes me feel emotional, and I still have my moments every week, but compared to how I was six months ago, I am now able to not cry every minute of every day. I don't have nightmares every night or just sit on the sofa, scrunched up and feeling nothing but hopeless. You learn to live with the situation that you are left with.

But everyone is different, and I'm just taking each day as it comes.

There is no time limit to grief, so take your time.

My tips for coping with grief at holidays

1- Acknowledge that the holidays will be different, tough and hard.

2- Light a candle in remembrance of the person you've lost.

3- Plan ahead and communicate with those you wish to spend the day with. For example, Dad and I had spoken about and planned what we were doing for Mum's birthday throughout the day.

4- The money you would have spent on gifts for your loved one, use that money to buy yourself a little something. Flowers? That new gadget you've been wanting for ages? Treat yourself. We need to think of ourselves too, and just that little something will make that day just that little bit easier. If you don't know what to get yourself then maybe donate the money to your chosen charity.

5- Create a new tradition in memory of your loved one.

6- Remember everyone around you will grieve differently.

7- Include one of your loved one's favourite meals on the day.

8- Play your loved one's favourite music.

9- Make a memory table and put out some of your favourite photos of your loved one.

10- Support the children around you and make a memorial grief activity together, for example, my daughter always makes a card for Mum and sometimes we do a painting of her too.

Remember, it's okay to be happy on these occasions too. It doesn't lessen the love we have or how much we really miss our loved ones who aren't here on the special holidays. Don't feel guilty – we deserve to be happy after all the sadness and pain we're going through.

CHAPTER TWENTY

The Weight Of Grief

"When someone you love dies, and you're not expecting it, you don't lose her all at once; you lose her in pieces over a long time — the way the mail stops coming, and her scent fades from the pillows and even from the clothes in her closet and drawers. Gradually, you accumulate the parts of her that are gone. Just when the day comes — when there's a particular missing part that overwhelms you with the feeling that she's gone, forever — there comes another day, and another specifically missing part." - John Irving

When you are mourning a loved one, it makes you feel so internally heavy and causes a huge strain on your mind and heart.

It's like wearing one of those oversized backpacks your mum made you wear on your first day at school, but the rucksack is filled with heavy rocks. Now, imagine carrying that rucksack full of rocks everywhere you go, stumbling around like a baby calf. It's so heavy that it makes every single part of your body sore. Eventually, over time, you decide to put it down for a minute, like you're waiting for your bus. And then the next minute that bus arrives and you're carrying that heavy rucksack again. Some days are more cope-able than others, and other days are so hard you can barely lift yourself up from the ground. But you do it, because you have to. The world goes on, and unfortunately without your loved one.

In my case, I wasn't just carrying the weight of my own grief, but I was also keeping my family together whilst they were grieving too.

Dad was so weak and depressed when Mum died, he didn't want to do anything – whether it was cooking, cleaning, doing his normal daily tasks, or even just interacting with us. He had gotten to a really dark place where he'd stay in bed all day and not get up, or if he did get up, he would be in an awfully foul mood – he'd come downstairs for a short while, rage at every little thing and then go back upstairs to his room.

I was left to take care of my brothers as well as my own daughter and it was hard, really really hard. It was a lot of pressure and responsibility shoved onto one person. And I would often stress and overthink when Dad would spit the words "I don't want to live anymore" to me.

I would constantly worry about my dad's health when he'd express how much pain he was in and that he just didn't want to be alive. I would tell him over and over again, reminding him that if he left us then I would be stressed out too, that we'd all be alone and that losing him wouldn't make things better. We had already lost Mum, I didn't want to lose Dad too.

I find that it's a lot harder to deal with my feelings at night time because it's dark, quiet and everyone's asleep, except me and my thoughts. It's hard to think of all the happy, good times when you're sat there, crying and trying to process everything.

I salute you if you are getting out of bed every morning, carrying that big heavy rucksack with you. Doing those house chores that you've been longing to do, paying those bills, doing the school run. Anything you do in your life whilst grieving. It takes a lot of courage to do that, YOU ARE AMAZING.

Please remember that it's okay to not be okay. It's okay to stay in bed sometimes, to grieve and be alone. It's okay to not do your daily tasks. Always make time for yourself, but if you feel as if you aren't coping, then please reach out to someone.

CHAPTER TWENTY-ONE

The Grief Cycle

Grief Lesson # 19:
It's okay to not be okay.

"Grief is the price we pay for love." Queen Elizabeth

The grieving process isn't as simple as we all think it's going to pan out to be. In my experience, it has been unpredictable, messy and like a total roller-coaster. It has been just over a year now since Mum passed away and I am now able to explain and discuss my stages and experiences with you, in the hope that this may help some of you.

Everyone grieves differently, and stages can come in any order, but this was what I personally experienced.

Denial

The first stage of my grief was denial. The moment the police told us that Mum had in fact passed away, I just couldn't believe it. In my head, I kept saying to myself that she's not gone and I'd expect my mum to walk through the door any second. It was only from the moment I saw Mum in her coffin at the funeral home that I started to believe and realise that she wasn't alive anymore and most definitely wasn't coming back. My mind had been so convinced that she had just packed her bag and gone to stay somewhere, it was just such a shock.

Depression

The second stage was depression, which came very soon after being in denial about my mum's death. I had no motivation to do anything, just sitting in the corner of the sofa, scrunched up into a little ball, staring into the distance like my mind was completely blank. I didn't have an appetite at all either, the thought of food would make me feel sick and gag in the first days after Mum's passing. All the goals I had in life before my mum passed away had been forgotten and thrown to the bin in my head. My biggest goal was to become a midwife and my mum would have been so supportive and excited for me, helping me think of goals I'd need to achieve first before getting to do midwifery. But now I don't want to do midwifery, the thought of it doesn't excite me anymore which is a real shame.

A couple of months after Mum died I started a blog about losing Mum to suicide. A lot of people messaged me and thanked me for sharing my experience. One person said: "Beautiful and touching write-up!!! I truly understand how it feels when your Mom leaves you for the heavens suddenly… I lost my mother on the 2nd January and I was not even able to say goodbye to her. Your Mom would be very proud of you, so take care and keep writing."

Another said: "lost my dad two months ago, not to suicide but ill health. Some of the things you said resonated with me. Especially thinking that she'll just walk through the door and it's not actually happened. I saw my dad die and I honestly still don't believe it. My thoughts are with you. Such a touching post x"

Reading these comments brought comfort to me in many ways, making me feel that I wasn't alone in this awful nightmare. At one point I thought I could maybe become a mental health support worker. I did so much research about this and then came to the conclusion that it wouldn't be possible for me in this moment of time, it's still so very raw and I could just imagine myself crying with the person I'd be helping which would not help at all.

In the fresh, early days I would occasionally have moments where I'd laugh at something or smile, then I would instantly feel bad for doing so and that smile would be swiped off my face straightaway. I would feel like I didn't deserve to be happy because Mum wasn't happy and now she's gone, so why should I ever be happy? It was almost like I was trying to punish myself.

Mum was the person who always had everything planned out, and all of our lives felt out of place without her. It still feels odd not having Mum here anymore, especially when it comes to special occasions and events, because we'd have those special times together as a family. But over time, we have adjusted to the new norm. My happiness was constantly drained. The grief ate me away bit by bit. I would feel so guilty about smiling, laughing, eating,

anything. I'd sit in the corner of the sofa just staring at the
TV, but I wouldn't be taking any notice of what was
actually going on, talking to myself in my head, saying how
awful life was, how could we ever be happy after this? I
really thought being happy again wouldn't be possible.

Shock

The third stage I experienced was shock. Every day, up
until I saw my mum in her coffin, I was so shocked and
didn't believe that she was gone. Shocked that she could
ever do this, that she could leave us. She showed us how
much she loved us every day. It was painful and so hard to
accept the fact that she had passed away. There will always
be a piece missing in my heart.

Some days it still shocks me. I'll have moments where I'll
reach for my phone to call her and then think, "Oh shoot,
she's not here anymore". Sometimes it just doesn't feel real.
It's crazy how one day your life is so normal and you're
content with how your life is and then the next day your
world gets turned upside down and you have to adjust to
this whole new routine. I still feel out of place at times but
writing this book has helped me a lot. To me, this is like
going to a support group.

When I saw my mum in her coffin, I felt numb and I
couldn't cry, and I felt so guilty because I wasn't able to cry
when I saw her, but then when I got home or when I was
on my own, it was like all my emotions would hit me at
once and it would become so real. I remember the day after
my mum passed away, I tried to distract myself by cleaning,
then all of a sudden a wave of heavy sadness hit me so
hard. Sometimes it felt like my heart was going to jump out
of my chest and that a huge golf ball was jammed in my
throat. Most days I honestly felt like my body was in the

room and I wasn't. I felt so worthless and no thoughts would go through my mind, like I was completely numb, a ghost in the room.

Anger

The fourth stage was anger, followed by bargaining. I experienced this around two months after my mum's death. I had many rows with my dad, brothers and even my partner. I'd get angry about absolutely anything. The slightest thing would send me over the edge, and even today, I still have little moments of becoming overwhelmed and losing it over something so minor.

I would think a lot about the night my mum passed away, and I'd think about how my mum's friend could have saved her by telling someone about her taking pills. Or I'd get angry at myself for not noticing the signs before it was too late. I'd feel so angry that Mum didn't leave us a note, but left a voicemail on her friend's phone. I'd think, "If she had just told us, we could have helped her!" It also broke my heart how my mum didn't feel like she could talk to me or my dad about how she was feeling, and that's why I feel like the only person who had an opportunity to save her was her friend. But my dad and I have discussed if any of us could have stopped her and in reality, even if we were able to, it would have probably only delayed her from trying to do it again.

Acceptance

The fifth stage which I have gradually gotten to is acceptance and if I didn't have family around me then I don't think I would have gotten this far to be honest. It's sort of a relief to be able to accept that my mum has passed away. I am fortunate that I was able to spend 22 years making incredible memories with my mum. I am blessed with everything she did for us all and all the memories we have with her. We have so many videos and photos of our mum and when the time is right, I will be able to go through them all and just remember the person she was, with her cheeky laughs and smiles. I even miss her moaning, haha!

I actually feel like if it wasn't for COVID and lockdown, I probably wouldn't have been able to grieve properly. Having to stay home and be isolated with my feelings and emotions in the first lockdown really did get to me, and I went through a very dark time, especially being a few weeks pregnant too. When Boris announced the lockdown, I had a very strange feeling – it was like a suffocated feeling and I felt homesick in my own home, if that makes sense? I wanted to be closer to Mum so I stayed with my dad for about a month until I felt better and able to come back to my own home. If COVID had never happened, I would have probably thrown myself into a job and pushed my grief to the back of my mind, leaving it there to deal with another day. You have to go through all the emotions and feelings otherwise it will come back to bite you, hard.

Don't get me wrong, I do still get days when the emotions creep up on me, the grief speaking to me in my head like, "Oh you look happy, listening to Lewis Capaldi, guess what? MUM!" Then I'm an emotional wreck and back to square one again for the next couple of days.

Grief doesn't have a time limit, it will always be there.

CHAPTER TWENTY-TWO

Top Tips For Non-Grievers

Death is uncontrollable. Although we will all leave this world one day, it just never gets easier for someone who loses a loved one.

Of course it's really common for people to pay their respects when they come across an announcement on social media of someone's loved one who's died. Although everyone grieves differently, there are things you can do that will help.

Whether you are a friend or a family member or you just know someone who is grieving, as someone who has experienced grief, I thought I'd provide some tips that I advise keeping in mind to help someone else who is going through a difficult time.

I too am guilty of doing some of these things prior to losing Mum – you don't realise how your words can affect someone else, but it's okay, that's why I have come up with some tips for you.

- Do not ask a griever how or when their loved one died. The amount of times I was asked how Mum passed away seconds after I had announced it on social media really ticked me off. Like, I had literally announced seconds ago that my mum had died and the first thing you thought to say was, "Oh my god, how did she die?!" Instead, consider saying, "I'm so sorry for your loss" or "Sending my condolences through these hard times."

- Do listen to the griever and offer your support if they need to talk. You don't have to have answers or say anything back, we just want to be heard and to release that intense pressure that we constantly feel. A lot goes through your head when you are grieving. I would often bottle my thoughts up in my head because I either didn't want to upset my dad with how I was feeling because he was already feeling so upset, or I felt like my partner was fed up with hearing about death. But when I was asked how I was feeling I would pour out my emotions, and it would be a huge sigh of relief to get it off my chest and it was a good feeling to know I was being listened to.

- Do not reassure us with sayings like, "They're in a better place now" or "Time is a great healer". Although you may mean well, these things are better left unsaid. They don't make us feel any better.

- Do not assume that we will be happier within months and not need any more support because everyone's grieving process is different. It can take years for life to adjust to a new normal routine and to find a happy place again. It's been just over a year since my mum died and I still get a lot of moments when I'm thrown down that dark hole again.

- Acknowledge our loss. Since Mum died I've noticed many people avoiding the whole Mum topic, like they're too scared to say her name. Almost as if everyone around you is treading on egg shells. Please don't be afraid of upsetting us, we want to talk about them – although it's sad, it's also comforting to be able to speak about our loved ones. If you don't know what to say then maybe start off by saying, "I've been thinking about you lately, want to meet up for a chat about your mum?" It's best to acknowledge these things instead of avoiding it.

- Do continue to check in on us and offer help. I know at times I felt that when Mum's funeral was over, some people who had been supporting us just left us like nothing had happened and expected us to reach out first. I always felt like a burden when I had to ask for help. If you do want to check in but are not quite sure how to approach someone who is grieving, just know that it doesn't have to be anything massive. You can help and ease some pressure from the griever by doing some of the following:

  - Offer to walk their dog

  - Offer to take their kids out to the park for a couple of hours

  - Help with their housework/anything that needs doing like ironing, washing laundry etc

  - Water the plants in their garden

  - Buy them some essentials from the shop and make a little hamper

  - Order them a takeaway

  - Bring round a "thinking of you" card, flowers, a homemade meal, snacks.

It can be absolutely anything.

But before offering to help them with things such as walking their dog or doing household chores, give them a call first. The same goes for spontaneously buying them takeaway, bringing round flowers, meals etc – it's best to leave these things on their doorstep and knock before leaving. Because if you're not that close with the griever then the last thing they want to do is stand there feeling miserable and having to chit chat with someone else for ages. Although we appreciate it, it's really the last thing we want to be doing.

- Please stop saying things you do not mean. Quite a few people would say to me, "My thoughts are with you" or "Always here if you EVER need anything". Then when I would reach out, I wouldn't get a single response. Grieving is hard enough so the last thing we need is empty words of comfort. Instead, send a card, call us and willingly listen to how we are feeling.

- Remember the dates – there are two special dates that mean a lot to us grievers and that is our loved one's birthday and the anniversary of their death. It doesn't matter how many years pass by, these days are sacred. In the first year of the loss of your loved one, everyone remembers, but then after that it becomes less and less and everyone around you starts to forget. We don't expect you to memorise these dates, but it makes a big difference and means a lot to us as grievers when someone acknowledges our loved one's importance. It's nice to know that you remember. There's no need to do anything massive, just a simple message or a card to basically tell us, "I remember and I'm thinking of you on this difficult day" is enough.

There is one last thing I'd like to say before you close this book.

Spend more time with your friends and families.

Take more photos and videos with them.

Make more memories together.

Always check up on your loved ones, and be kind to one another. Every day, look out for those important signs. Don't make the same mistake that I made. Just always be wary. I am now forever wary of those around me, I'm always checking on them, day in and day out, making sure that they know I'm here for them.

Keep safe, Chloe xx

Printed in Great Britain
by Amazon